My friend thinks he is so smart.
He said onions are the only food
that makes you cry.
So I threw a coconut on his face.

- Anonymous

I hope that you have as much fun with this book
as we had when we created it!
I would also be grateful if you'd post a short review on Amazon.
Your support really does make a difference and I always read
the reviews personally so I can get your feedback and make
this book, and the ones to follow, even better.
Thanks again for your support!
To get even more recipes that aren't included here,
please sign up at destinationflorida.com
Cheers,
Pamela Childs

Special thanks to all of the talented chefs and wonderful restaurants who contributed to this compilation of fabulous recipes from the Florida Keys & Key West. You're the best!

Copyright © 2020
Pamela A. Childs

All Rights Reserved.
Published in the United States of America

No part of this book may be used or reproduced by any means, graphic, electronic, or mechanical, including photocopying, recording, taping, or by any information storage retrieval system without the written permission of the publisher except in the case of brief quotations embodied in critical articles and reviews.

ISBN 978-1-7358255-0-2

Pamela A. Childs
PO Box 1233 | Key West, Fl 33041

SO, WHAT EXACTLY IS "FLORIDA KEYS CUISINE?"
4 - 5   A Short Primer

HOW TO USE THIS BOOK
6   It doesn't matter whether you like to cook or not!

HANDHELDS & LITE BITES
8   *Fresh Fish, No Frills:* Key Largo Fisheries
9   Shrimp Burger
10 *Catch of the Day:* Reel Burger
11 King Crab Burger
12 Conch Egg Rolls
13 Conch Ceviche
14 *Think Outside the Salad Bowl:* Olive Morada
15 Espresso Balsamic Glazed Bacon
16 Shaved Conch Salad
17 *Socca:* A Moveable Feast
18 *Three Joints Are Better Than One:* Square Grouper
19 Oysters Rockefeller
20 *The Pulse of Islamorada:* Lorelei Restaurant & Cabana Bar
21 Keys Conch Chowder
22 *Real Barbeque:* Porky's Bayside
23 Smoked Fish Dip
24 *Key West's Sushi Ninja:* Ambrosia Sushi Restaurant
25 Spicy Tuna Tartare
26 *Master Chef John Correa:* Cafe Sole
27 Conch Carpaccio
28 *Right On The Dock:* Bistro 245
29 Island Gazpacho
30 Burrata Cheese with Balsamic Strawberry Sauce

's Cookin'?

32   *It's all about Romance:* Latitudes Restaurant

MAIN EVENTS
34   *Tiki Chic:* Snooks Bayside
35   *Yellowtail Snapper Encrusted with Citrus Zest*
36   *Something to Crow About:* The Buzzard's Roost
37   *Chipotle Glazed Mahi Mahi*
38   *Fresh Off the Boat:* Fish House Restaurant
39   Fish Matecumbe
40   Braised Short Ribs
41   Pina Colada Shrimp
42   Bacon Wrapped Love
44   *Legendary Food & a Storied Past:* Ziggie & Mad Dog's
45   Honey Grilled Chicken
46   *Life's a Beach:* Lazy Days
47   Fish with Key Lime Butter Sauce
48   *Puttin' on the Dog:* Ciao Hound
49   Frutti Di Mare
50   *The People Have Spoken:* Key Colony Inn
51   Scallops New Brunswick
52   *Pete the Greek:* 7 Mile Grill
53   Shrimp Saganaki
54   *A Last Little Piece of Old Key West:* Schooner Wharf
55   Filet Mignon, Island Style
56   *Honey Citrus Glazed Salmon:* Lighthouse Grill
57   *Cilantro-Seared Swordfish:* Tavern N Town
58   *Jonesing for Terrific Pasta:* Mangia Mangia
59   Rigatoni with Jumbo Shrimp

60   *Fried Chicken with Island Key Lime Sour Orange:* Bahama Village
61   *Island Shrimp Cakes:* Square Grouper
72   *Tako - Yakini Ku:* Kaiyo Grill & Sushi

SWEET TREATS
64   *Kristi's Tropical Rum Cake:* Olive Morada
65   *Easy Peasy Creamy Mango Pie:* Mango Fest
66   *Key Lime Pie Addict,* David Sloan
67   *Authentic Key Lime Pie:* Pepe's Cafe
68   *Banana Bread:* Lazy Lobster
69   *Puffins Pancake Mini-Muffins:* Firefly Key West

FOODIE HAPPENINGS IN THE KEYS
70-73   Your Month-by-Month Guide
74   Uncorked! Key Largo & Islamorada Food & Wine Festival
75   Key West Food & Wine Festival
76   Original Marathon Seafood Festival
77   Florida Keys Island Fest
78   Mango Fest Key West
79   Key West's Key Lime Festival
80   Key West Lobsterfest

KEYS EATS
81-85   Upper Keys Restaurants
85-89   Marathon/Middle Keys Restaurants
89-98   Key West Restaurants

INDEX
99-100   Where to Find What

ABOUT THE AUTHOR
101   Pamela Childs

So What Exactly is "Florida Keys Cuisine?"

It's spicy conch chowder, savory Cuban pork, succulent pink shrimp dipped in tangy mustard sauce, or coated in coconut. And it's all as unique and appealing as the 125-mile island chain itself.

The Keys have a rich seafaring history (even today, fishing remains the second largest industry here), so you'll find lots of it on local menus including yellowtail, grouper, mutton snapper, and Mahi-mahi which are generally sautéed, broiled or blackened.

Ever hear of Key West pink shrimp? Considered one of the Keys' most popular "natural resources," it's a bit sweeter than other types of shrimp and can be sautéed, battered and fried, used on salad and pasta, or steamed and served with savory sauces.

If you happen to come down during "Stone Crab Season" (October 15 - May 15), you're really in luck. Stone crab claws, renowned for their sweet and succulent meat, are a popular delicacy here. They can be served warm with drawn butter or chilled with mustard sauce.

Just be careful because either way, they are totally addictive.

We have lobster down here, too, but unlike its northern cousin, our spiny lobster is clawless. The meat, however, is still sweet and tender, and just like a "Maine" lobster, it's often served steamed or broiled with drawn butter.

Conch (pronounced "konk") is another delicacy for your foodie bucket list. Even though

it's no longer fished in the Keys (most of it comes in from the Bahamas), you'll still find it on a lot of local menus. This versatile mollusk pops up in spicy tomato-based chowder, deep-fried fritters, ceviche, and even breaded and fried as conch steak. No two restaurants prepare conch precisely the same way, and we've included several recipes for you to enjoy on pages 12, 13, 16, 21, and 27.

Of course, it's no surprise that the most popular ethnic food in the Keys is Cuban, brought to Key West by the cigar makers and their families who fled their homeland in the 1800s. Cuban dishes include Ropa Vieja (a rustic, humble stew with shredded beef in red sauce); Picadillo (a soft, fragrant stew of ground beef and tomatoes); and the biggest crowd-pleaser of all: The Cuban mix sandwich—

a blend of slow-roasted pork, ham, Swiss cheese, and pickles served on fresh Cuban bread, flattened in a press that looks like a waffle iron. There are several excellent Cuban restaurants throughout the Keys, and we've listed our favorites on pages 93.

Oh, and let's not forget the Keys' signature dessert: Key lime pie. Believe it or not, no two Key lime pie recipes

are alike. Some are topped with meringue and some with whipped cream. Some are nestled in a graham cracker crust, while others rest in a chocolate crust. We've included a recipe for one of our favorite versions that you can try at home on page 67.

If you get down to the Keys, we encourage you to make the rounds and taste as many as possible so you can discover your personal favorite.

Chow!

Special thanks to fla-keys.com

How to Use this Book

I*'m guessing that you like to cook, or you wouldn't be reading this compilation of great recipes that I've collected from some of the best restaurants in the Florida Keys & Key West.

Truth be told: it doesn't matter if you like to cook or not. This "Keys Keepsake Cookbook" is more of a foodie travel guide that takes you on a flavorful romp from Key Largo to Key West.

If you can get down to the Keys, by all means, please do! That way, you can plan a trip around the featured restaurants and order your favorite dishes right from the source.

Oh, and if you do go, please be sure to take along your copy of "Keys Eats," so that you can make any special notations, and have the featured chefs and restauranteurs autograph it. Heck, you might even garner some VIP treatment!

BTW: Grab your calendar — because in the back of the book, you'll find a handy guide to a whole bunch of fun food-related events that take place throughout the year.

I've also included a comprehensive list of great local restaurants. Take special note of the little red compass that appears among the listings. It delineates some of my personal favorites. You can use these recommendations as the starting point for creating your own personal "favorite digs" list. Once you've chatted with some of the other locals down here, follow your nose and start your Keys adventure!

Enjoy!

Fresh Fish, No Frills
KEY LARGO FISHERIES BACKYARD CAFE

Until a few years back, we always thought there was nothing like a great Maine lobster roll. Of course that was before we stumbled upon the Backyard Cafe on the docks behind Key Largo Fisheries and discovered their signature Lobster BLT.

Perfectly cooked, firm-tender lobster (not fried - Sacre Bleu!) is generously heaped on a buttery Croissant fused with crisp bacon, juicy ripe tomato slices, fresh Bibb lettuce and a healthy slather of spicy mayo.

This is a family-owned business that has been feeding customers fresh seafood since 2011 but the Fisheries itself has a history that goes all the way back to 1972 when Jack and Dottie Hill operated a small fishing ground where local fishermen sold their catches.

Four generations later, the Hill family still owns and operates Key Largo Fisheries. As a real, working dock and fishing ground, fishing boats pull to their docks and unload their catches right next to the popular waterfront Backyard Cafe. The boat-to-table seafood is then processed right on the premises before being served at the cafe, sold in their own retail market or shipped all over the country.

This is truly a great place where you can experience a working waterfront and literally buy seafood just off the boat. Best of all, it won't break the bank. A family of four can get a terrific meal for less than a hundred bucks.

You can find the Backyard Cafe on the dock behind Keys Fisheries, 1313 Ocean Bay Drive, Key Largo 33037. Info: 305-451-3782; keylargofisheries.com.

SHRIMP BURGER

Key Largo Fisheries

This delightful open air cafe is located on one of Key Largo's most scenic working waterfronts and the seafood here literally comes right off the boats docked next to the restaurant.

SHRIMP BURGER INGREDIENTS
(Yield 4 Servings)
1-¼ Lbs Key West pink shrimp, cleaned and diced
4 Medium Eggs, beaten
8 Tbl Fine Panko
2 Tbl Flour
1 Tsp Garlic Powder
4 Tsp Parsley Flakes
1 Tsp Thyme
Salt and pepper to taste
1 Cup Pico de Gallo (recipe follows)
3-4 Tbl Butter, for sautéing shrimp cake
4 French Rolls
Lettuce and Tomato for garnish

PREPARATION:
Mix the diced shrimp with the egg, panko and flour. Add garlic powder, parsley flakes, thyme, pico de gallo. Salt and pepper to taste. Mix well. Mixture should be "pasty" and hold together like a patty. If it is too wet, add a small amount of panko until the desired consistency is achieved. Prepare 4 patties, and set aside. Place a sauté pan on the stove over medium high heat. Add butter for sautéing. Once butter melts, add the shrimp cakes to the sauté pan and sauté for about 4 minutes per side or until the internal temperature reaches 165° Remove from sauté pan and serve on toasted French rolls. Garnish with lettuce and tomato and fresh pico de gallo.

PICO DE GALLO INGREDIENTS:
1 Ripe Tomato, diced
¼ Red Onion, diced
¼ Red Bell Pepper, diced
1 Jalapeño, seeded and diced
4 Key Limes, juiced
Pinch of Cayenne Pepper
1 Tbl Cilantro, chopped
Salt and pepper to taste

PREPARATION:
Place tomatoes, onions, bell pepper and jalapeño into a small bowl. Mix well. Add lime juice, spices, and chopped cilantro. Mix well.

You can find Key Largo Fisheries at 1313 Ocean Bay Drive in Key Largo.
Info: 305.451.3782; KeyLargoFisheries.com

Catch of The Day –
REEL BURGER IN PARADISE

Here in the Keys, we've got it all: Black Angus steaks. Fresh-off-the-boat seafood. Gourmet Italian. Authentic Mexican. Thai and sushi. You name it, and we'll point you in the right direction.

But sometimes, just sometimes, what you're really hankering for is a burger. And not just any burger. It's gotta be a big, fat, juicy, two-fisted, beefy monster that etiquette gurus like Emily Post would have you eating with a knife and fork.

When that urge hits, grab your flip flops and head over to Reel Burger at Islamorada's Amara Cay Resort. Backdropped by the sun-speckled Atlantic and majestic island palms, Reel Burger's Tiki Bar is a breezy poolside spot, where an all-day menu includes seven signature burgers, big salad "Burger Bowls" and "Social Beginnings" with lighter bites like Fish Tacos, Cheesy Chili Nachos and Grilled Honey Habanero Wings.

But it's those epicurean burger creations, made with a unique blend of brisket and prime beef, that'll hook you every time.

Our favorite: "The Attitude Burger." Coated with smoked cheddar, tomato jam, Applewood bacon and fresh greens, this Yummer barely fits on the freshly toasted brioche bun that it's cuddled between.

If red meat "ain't your thang," you can always opt for the "Tree Hugger," a house-made vegetarian burger with crisp greens, grilled portobello, melted provolone, tomato, red onion, avocado and spicy mayo on toasted brioche. There's also the "Hot Chick": grilled, cilantro-marinated chicken breast, provolone, roasted tomato, artisan field greens, avocado and red onion with a zing of Sriracha mayo.

The craftsmanship continues behind the bar, as well, with a whole lot of tiki and craft cocktails, specialty shakes, beer and premium wine.

You can find Reel Burger at Amara Cay Resort, MM 80, Oceanside. Open 11:30am - 10pm. Info: 305-664-0073; amaracayresort.com.

KING CRAB BURGER
Reel Burger & Tiki Bar, Islamorada

Reel Burger at Amara Cay Resort is one of Islamorada's favorite spots for made-to-order, handcrafted burgers, crispy house fries, frothy milkshakes and specialty cocktails. From simple burgers to signature custom blends like this King Crab Burger, it's a perfect spot to kick back and get your tiki on!

INGREDIENTS
(Yield 4 Servings)
2 Lbs Alaskan king crab
1 Red Bell Pepper - diced
1 Green Bell Pepper - diced
1 Fresh Squeezed Lime
¼ Cup Mayonnaise
¼ Cup Panko Bread Crumbs
1 Tsp Chopped Cilantro
Salt & Pepper to taste
½ Tsp Old Bay Seasoning
1 Small Shallot - diced
Olive Oil

1 Tomato - sliced
1 Avocado - sliced
4 Large Lettuce Leaves
4 Fresh Hamburger Buns

PREPARATION
Squeeze king crab meat to remove excess liquid. Add all ingredients in a large bowl and mix together gently. Let mixture set for 2 hours. Mold 4 patties. Heat olive oil on cast iron skillet on medium before placing patties. Cook each side until golden brown. Toast buns and build your burger. Yum!

You can find at Reel Burger located at the oceanfront Amara Cay Resort, 80001 Overseas Hwy, Islamorada. 305-664-0073; AmaraCayResort.com

CONCH EGG ROLLS
with Key Lime-Wasabi Aioli

Mile Marker 88, Islamorada

Locals have been hanging out at this popular waterfront eatery since the late '60's. Here's the recipe for one of our favorite apps.

INGREDIENTS FOR EGG ROLLS
(Yield 6 Servings)
3 Egg Yolks
1/2 Lb ground conch
1 Head Japanese cabbage
1 Carrot, shredded
1 Tbl Soy Sauce
2 Tbl White Wine
1/4 Head Radicchio
12 Spring Roll Wrappers
Oil for frying
Salt & Pepper to taste

DIRECTIONS FOR EGG ROLLS
Sauté conch with soy sauce, white wine, salt and pepper. Cook for 5 minutes, then strain and save liquid. Set aside to drain and cool to room temperature. Cook cabbage and carrots in pan with liquid. Cook until vegetables are covered with liquid and just begin to wilt. Strain and discard liquid. Set aside to cool to room temperature and dry vegetables once cool, by wringing out vegetables in a cheesecloth or a clean kitchen towel.

Combine conch and vegetables and place 1 1/2 - 2 tablespoons of mixture in the center of spring roll wrapper and roll into an egg roll shape. "Seal" top edge of egg roll by moistening inside top corner of the spring roll wrapper with egg yolks. Chill egg rolls for at least 30 minutes in refrigerator before frying. Fry until golden brown.

INGREDIENTS FOR THE KEY LIME AIOLI
5 Large Egg Yolks
6 Garlic Cloves, peeled and pressed
1/3 Tsp Salt
2 Key Limes, juiced
1 Cup Vegetable Oil
Ground White Pepper
1 Key Lime, Zested
2 Tbl Prepared Wasabi

DIRECTIONS FOR THE KEY LIME AIOLI
Place all ingredients (except oil) in food processor or blender and blend well. Slowly incorporate oil. Mix until aioli achieves the desired consistency. Mix in the prepared wasabi to taste.

You can find Marker 88 at 88000 Overseas Hwy, Islamorada, (MM 88, Bayside) 305-852-9315; info@marker88.info

CONCH CEVICHE
Celebrity Chef, Alice Weingarten, Key West

When celebrated Florida chef, Alice Weingarten, steps into the kitchen, watch out because you're in for some seriously wonderful food. Her conch ceviche is a total knock out!

INGREDIENTS
(Yield 4 Servings)
2 lbs fresh Conch – cleaned and diced
1/4 cup small diced green peppers
1/4 cup small diced red peppers
2 tbl chopped fresh cilantro
1 cup fresh lime juice
1 tbl Siracha (Asian Hot Sauce)
1/2 tsp sea salt or kosher salt
1/4 tsp fresh ground black pepper

PREPERATION
Rinse conch steaks under cold water until surface is smooth and water runs clear. Dice Conch into small pieces. Note: Conch is easier to handle and cut if it's slightly frozen.

Place diced Conch meat, peppers and chopped cilantro in a bowl. Add fresh lime juice, Siracha, salt and pepper. Toss until lime juice has evenly coated all ingredients. Cover bowl and chill for 45 minutes to an hour.

Alice's Tip For Jazzing Things Up: Add fresh small shrimp and bay scallops prior to adding lime juice. With the Conch meat, the acid in the lime juice will cook the scallops and shrimp. Add a shooter of Gazpacho on the side for a cooling touch.

Think Outside the Salad Bowl!

OLIVE MORADA, ISLAMORADA

1f you haven't noticed, olive oil and balsamic vinegar are not just for salads anymore. Infused versions are showing up in everything from seafood, beef and poultry dishes to soups, cakes and cocktails.

Maybe it's because food just seems to taste better with a little drizzle, and because with the right combination of infused oil and balsamic you can truly enhance any culinary creation.

And that brings us to a nifty little shop called Olive Morada.

Located in the heart of Islamorada, Florida, Olive Morada carries 45 flavors of infused oils and vinegars — all handcrafted from the freshest imported Extra Virgin Olive Oils and Vinegars.

Extra virgin olive oil is considered the best or premium of the olive oils. Why?

Because virgin olive oil is made using a mechanical cold pressing process which produces the "extra" in its production as long as the oleic acid is less than one percent free.

Now imagine taking these two wonderful condiments and adding an array of aromatic and appetizing infusions that can be paired together in hundreds of different ways.

It may sound a bit daunting but Olive Morada takes away all the guesswork. Their unique Tasting Bar gives you an opportunity to experience the taste and aroma of a variety of fabulously fresh olive oils and balsamic vinegars.

Whether you are a professional chef, casual cook or foodie, Owner and Master Mixologist, Jen White, can help unleash your culinary genius and show you infinite combinations of olive oil and balsamic vinegars for use in salads, marinades, desserts, beverages and more.

In fact, she also has tons of great recipes to share using combinations like Persian Lime Olive Oil & Coconut Balsamic to create a delicious Tropical Rum Cake; Blood Orange Olive Oil & Vanilla Balsamic to whip up a yummy batch of Balsamic Sweet Potatoes; and Pineapple & Cranberry Pear Balsamic to shake up a mean Citrus Balsamic Punch.

Sound cool? Then hit the road and get a taste of the fun flavors of Olive Morada.

FYI: In addition to selling full size bottles of her infused oils and balsamics, Jen also stocks sample packs along with a really great collection of gourmet foods and spices, gift baskets and accessories, Next time you're in the Keys, stop by Olive Morada at 82245 Overseas Hwy, Islamorada, Fl. You can also check them out at olivemorada.com. Info: 305-735-4375

ESPRESSO BALSAMIC GLAZED BACON

Olive Morada, Islamorada

If there was ever such a thing as legal crack, we think that espresso balsamic glazed bacon would be it. One thing's for sure: it's totally addictive. So addictive, in fact, that we could not stop shoveling these sweet, savory strips into our mouths. If you need a new party trick or you're just a bacon fanatic, this recipe is for you.

INGREDIENTS
(Yield 6 Servings)
12 Oz Package Thick Cut Bacon
1-1/2 - 2 Tbl Espresso Coffee
1/2 Cup Olive Morada's Dark Espresso Balsamic Vinegar

PREPARATION:
Preheat oven to 425 degrees. Lay bacon slices on a rack over a sheet pan. Season both sides of bacon with coffee rub, and brush both sides with a nice coating of Olive Morada's Espresso Balsamic Vinegar. Place in oven for approximately 15 minutes…turning once…or until bacon caramelizes. This will happen fairly quick because of the balsamic, so keep an eye on it. Serve alone, as a side to a delicious breakfast, or on top of a burger. *Delicious!*

For a complete selection of vinegars and olive oils, visit Olive Morada, 82245 Overseas Hwy, Islamorada. 305-735-4375; olivemorada.com

SHAVED CONCH SALAD
Tides Beachside Bar & Grill, Islamorada

A true "Island Boy," the Islander Resort's award-winning Executive Chef Andy Neidenthal, is a master at creating inventive "Florribean" dishes. His shaved conch salad is particularly good.

INGREDIENTS
(Yield 6 Servings)
3 Lbs Conch Fillet
2 Cups Key Lime Juice
2 Cups Orange Juice
1 Green Pepper, julienned
1 Red Pepper, julienned
1 Bunch Cilantro, chopped
1 Red Onion, diced
1 Bunch Scallions, chopped
1 Habanero Pepper, seeded & minced
1/2 Cup Olive Oil
3 Cloves Garlic, chopped
1 Cucumber - ruffled
Salt & Pepper to taste

PREPARATION:
Thinly shave well-chilled Conch. Place in non-reactive bowl with all citrus juices and let stand for 20 minutes. Add remaining ingredients and season with salt and pepper to taste. Served well chilled with ruffle cucumber.

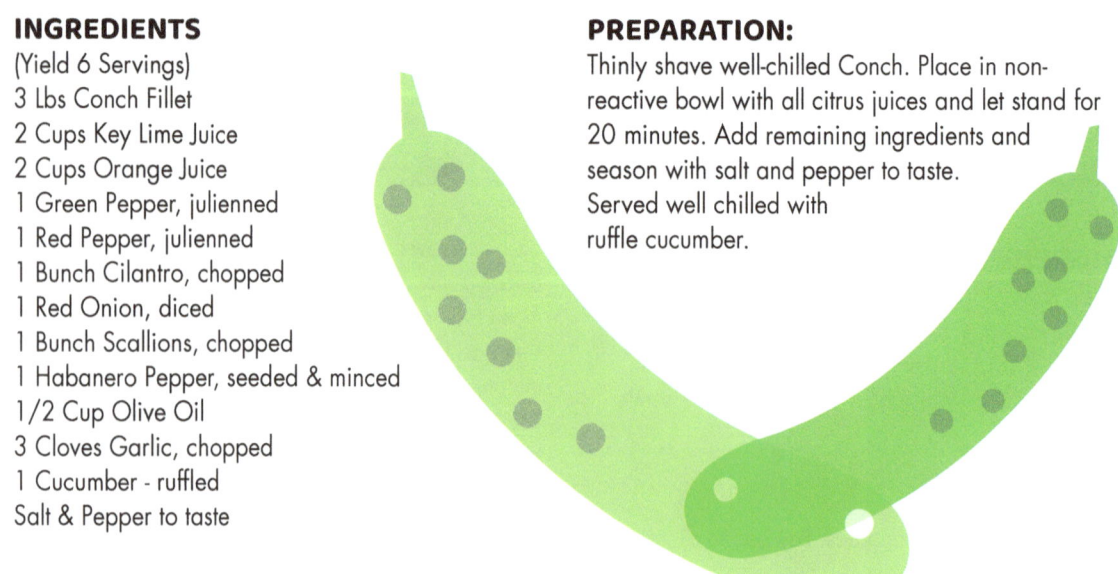

You can find Tides Beachside Bar & Grill at the Islander Resort, 82100 Overseas Hwy, (MM 81.4 Bayside) Islamorada. 305-664-6002; islamoradaislander.com

SOCCA

A Moveable Feast, Islamorada

Chef/Owners Tony and Marina Corallo take Food Truck dining to a whole new level. Unique creations like "Global" Tacos and "Gourmet" Grilled Cheese Sandwiches are creatively paired with familiar "comfort" ingredients and unique hand made sauces, salsas, chutneys, compotes and spice mixtures that result in amazing flavor combinations. We tried a "healthy-ish" item called Socca. These savory great tasting crepes, which are vegan as well as gluten-free, are served with sides of homemade kimchi, oven roasted garlic-tomato compote, Asian slaw, pickled red onions with jalapeño and ginger-cilantro aioli but you can pair them with just about any condiment, sauce or salsa.

INGREDIENTS
(Yield 2 Servings)
2 Cups Chickpea Flour
1/2 Tbl Dried Thyme
1/2 Tbl Rubbed Sage
1/2 Tbl Dried Oregano
1 Tsp Kosher Salt
2 Tbl Garlic Powder
1/2 Tsp Ground Cumin
1/2 Tsp Turmeric
1 Tbl Paprika
1 Tsp Chili Powder
1 Tbl Extra Virgin Olive Oil
Fresh Ground Black Pepper, to taste

PREPARATION
Blend all ingredients together in a food processor. Separate into 2.3 oz portions. Mix each portion with 5oz distilled water to create individual crepe batter. Preheat oven broiler. In a 9"or 10" non-stick sauté pan over medium high heat add the extra virgin olive oil and heat until it's shimmering but not smoking. Pour in crepe batter and cook until becomes dried around edges. Place pan under broiler until surface of crepe is browned and crispy. Remove from pan and repeat process for next crepe. Cut into slices and enjoy on their own or with your choice of condiment, sauce or salsa.

You can find this "Feast Beast" on wheels parked next to Florida Keys Brewing, 81611 Old Hwy, (MM 81.5 Oceanside) Islamorada. 305-304-0340; flkeysfoodtruck.com

Three Joints Are Better Than One
THE SQUARE GROUPER BAR & GRILL

With three thriving restaurants in Paradise, Keys' Restaurateur Lynn Bell is "livin' the dream" and ringing bells with food critics left and right.

So what's with the name? Derived from the 1980s drug-running era, "Square Grouper" refers to the bales of marijuana that were often found floating off the coast of Florida. The name may be funny, but don't be fooled. Square Grouper's food is seriously good. So good that Lynn's three hip roadside eateries always make the Keys Top 10 restaurant list.

Whether you go to the original Square Grouper on Cudjoe Key, upstairs to "My New Joint," Lynn's swanky tapas and classic cocktail hang, or to her newest waterfront addition, Square Grouper Islamorada, you can always expect the food to be consistently fantastic.

Menus for each location are a bit different but don't be surprised to see particular local favorites pop up at all locations. Our personal preferences include the Ahi Tuna Avocado Egg Rolls, Flash-Fried Conch, Homemade Smoked Fish Dip, and the Jasmine Rice Bowls with sweet Thai chili butter sauce, spinach and chopped cashews, packed with your choice of seafood, chicken or portabella mushroom.

Lynn's lineup of fresh local seafood, certified Angus steaks, and innovative daily creations always keep things interesting, but it's those damn "Magical Brownies" with ice cream, chocolate sauce, and Heath Bar Crunches that will put you over the moon. It's no wonder that the Square Grouper family is one of the Keys' favorite joints!

Find the Original Square Grouper and the upstairs, "My New Joint" at 22658 Overseas Hwy (MM 22, Oceanside) on Cudjoe Key. Info: 305-745-8880; squaregrouperbarandgrill.com. Square Grouper Islamorada is located on the Marina at 80460 Overseas Highway (MM 80.5, Bayside). Info: 786-901-5678; squaregrouperIslamorada.com.

OYSTERS ROCKEFELLER

Square Grouper, Islamorada

Considered to be one of the Keys' Top "Must Visit" restaurants, Square Grouper Bar & Grill has a reputation for innovative local seafood preparations, house-made desserts, eclectic boutique wines and unusual craft beer. Chef/owner Lynn Bell never ceases to amaze us with all of her fabulous specials. Here's the recipe:

INGREDIENTS
(Yield 1 Serving)
6 Large Shucked Oysters
2 Large Minced Shallots
2 Tbl Olive Oil
2 Cups Chablis White Wine
2 Cups Heavy Cream
1 Lb Fresh Spinach
1 Cup Key Lime Juice
1 Cup Grated Parmesan Cheese
1-1/2 Cup Panko Breadcrumbs
2 Tbl Salt & Pepper
2 Tbl Granulated Garlic
1/2 Cup Melted Butter
6 Lemon Wedges

PREPARATION FOR ROCKEFELLER MIXTURE
Heat oil over medium heat, add shallots and cook until translucent. Deglaze with chablis. Reduce until 50% of liquid remains in saucepan. Add spinach, heavy cream and key lime juice. Cook lightly until spinach is wilted and soft. Use immersion blender to combine ingredients. Mix until smooth and vibrant green. Add parmesan cheese and 1/2 cup of the Panko bread crumbs to thicken mixture and form a light paste. Add salt & pepper to taste.

PREPARATION FOR BREADCRUMB TOPPING
Toss remaining Panko crumbs with melted butter, granulated garlic and salt and pepper. Combine well.

SERVING INSTRUCTIONS
Pre-heat oven to 350°. Place the six oysters on the half shell onto an oiled sheet tray. Top each oyster with two tablespoons of Rockefeller mix. Place in 350° oven and cook for 5 minutes. Remove from oven and add one tablespoon of breadcrumb topping to each oyster. Broil for 90 seconds until a golden brown crust forms on the top of each oyster. Plate oysters and serve with lemon wedges. Enjoy!

You can find Square Grouper at MM 80.4, Bayside in Islamorada (786-901-5678) and at MM 22.5 on Cudjoe Key. 305-745-880; squaregrouperbarandgrill.com

The Pulse Of Islamorada
LORELEI RESTAURANT & CABANA BAR, ISLAMORADA

What began as a rustic 1940s Fishing Camp with only a dock, two folding chairs and an "honor system" beer cooler, is now one of Islamorada's most notorious restaurants and watering holes.

If you head south on the Overseas Highway, you can't miss the ginormous mermaid that marks the spot of the Lorelei - a sprawling bayside eatery and Cabana Bar where flip flops, fish tales and tropical cocktails are de rigueur.

You never know who you'll run into at this popular hotspot — especially during the daily Happy Hour from 4 - 6pm when well drinks are just three bucks and domestic drafts go for a buck and a half.

In fact, if you do a little eavesdropping at the bar, you're likely to hear a fishing boat captain talking about his day's charter with a stockbroker on his left, and a school teacher on his right.

And then there's the nightly "Sunset Celebration" when the live music kicks in and the bar crowd spills onto the beach for some serious toes-in-the sand revelry.

Partying aside, the Lorelei also serves up some really good fare and the menu, as expected, is full of island-style eats. You can make an entire meal out of just the appetizers which include homemade conch chowder, bacon-wrapped shrimp in Thai Chili Sauce, homemade Fish Dip, Tuna Nachos and Coconut Shrimp.

Topping the list of entrees: Florida Stone Crabs (in season) Alaskan Snow Crab, fresh local Snapper and Mahi-Mahi, Bahamian Conch, Steamboat Channel Shrimp, and warm water Lobster. The Surf-n-Turf and Key Lime Peppercorn Snapper are both especially good and the kitchen also serves an excellent Vegan Sauté dinner.

On Sundays, you can't beat Lorelei's Jamaican Jerk dinner special (Chicken, Pork, or a combo of both) for $12.95. Make sure to save room for dessert because their award-winning Key Lime Pie takes the cake. If you prefer to sip your dessert, the frozen Key Lime Colada drink is "Dessert in a cup" with a nice kick.

You can find this fun Keys institution at 81924 Overseas Hwy (Mile Marker 82 bayside), in the heart of Islamorada. Info: 305-664-2692 loreleicabanabar.com

KEYS CONCH CHOWDER
Lorelei Restaurant & Cabana Bar, Islamorada

Islamorada's favorite spot for celebrating sunset has a laid-back local vibe that inspires you to kick off your flip flops and wiggle your toes in the sand. The food here is tropical casual and includes lots of island specialties like this recipe for their homemade Conch Chowder.

INGREDIENTS
(Yield 3 Quarts)
1 Large Spanish Onion, coarsely chopped
1 Large Bell Pepper, coarsely chopped
1 Large Carrot, coarsely chopped
2 Whole Bay Leaves
2 Tbl Bacon fat
2 Tbl Fresh Chopped Garlic
2 Lbs Conch meat coarsely ground
2 Cups Canned Diced Tomatoes
7 Cups Canned/Bottled Clam Juice
1-3/4 Lbs Potatoes, coarsely chopped
1 Tbl Basil Leaves
2 Tsp Black Pepper
1 Tbl Oregano
1 Tbl Thyme
1 Tbl Cumin
1 Tsp Cayenne Pepper
1-¼ Tsp Salt
1 Tsp Tabasco Sauce

Note: Conch meat can be purchased from most local fish markets. Frozen ground clams can be substituted if conch is not available.

PREPARATION
In a large sauce pan, combine peppers, onions, carrots, garlic and bacon fat with bay leaves, tomatoes, clam juice and all other spices. Simmer for 45 minutes and then add potatoes and ground conch meat. Continue to simmer until potatoes thicken the chowder.

You can find the Lorelei Restaurant & Cabana Bar at 81924 Overseas Hwy, (MM 82, Bayside) in the heart of Islamorada. 305-664-2692; loreleicabanabar.com

Real Southern Barbeque –
PORKY'S BAYSIDE, MARATHON

If you want to experience the Keys the way they used to be, then head on over to Porky's Bayside in Marathon.

Originally known as Bill Thompson's Villa and Marina, it was the place to be in the 1950's and hosted all sorts of famous visitors including Ernest Hemingway, Jimmy Hoffa and Elizabeth Taylor.

Today, Porky's Bayside is still the place to be. Overlooking Capt. Pip's Marina & Hideaway at MM 47.5, Gulfside, this funky, open air restaurant and bar is a local favorite known for its roug-hewn waterfront setting, top live entertainment and real down home barbeque.

We're not talkin' Arby's here. When we say barbeque, we mean REAL BARBEQUE.

The kind of lip-smackin', finger-lickin' roll-up-your-sleeves barbeque that keeps you coming back for more.

You can order up Porky's famous Smokehouse BBQ Pork and Beef, North Carolina Hot Pepper Pulled Pork or Citrus Marinade Cuban Pork as a lumberjack-size sandwich or in a big basket with your choice of baked beans, french fries, coleslaw, corn on the cob or potato salad. For a buck more you can get sweet potato fries or onion rings.

The juicy Quarter Smokehouse Chicken and Quarter Rack of fall-off- the-bone spareribs are also a good bet and you can order those up separately or as a Dinner for Two with a choice of four side dishes.

Even if you aren't into down home barbeque, you'll totally enjoy the fresh local seafood at Porky's. Especially good is the Lobster Bisque, Asian Seared Sashimi Tuna, Gulfstream Mahi-Mahi and Florida Bay Jumbo Shrimp.

Whichever way you go, just be sure to save room for Porkys original Fried Key Lime Pie. It 's a total out-of-body experience that's worth every last calorie!

Open daily 8 a.m. - 10 p.m. Live music nightly. Beer and wine. Major credit cards.

Located at MM 47.5, Gulfside, Marathon. 305-289-2065.

SMOKED FISH DIP
Porky's Bayside, Marathon

Located in a funky waterfront Tiki hut just north of Marathon's famous 7 Mile Bridge, Porky's Bayside is notorious for the best barbecue in the Keys. Locals and visitors have been flocking here since the early 1950s including such notables as Ernest Hemingway, Jimmy Hoffa and Elizabeth Taylor. But Southern BBQ isn't the only big draw here. They also serve up terrific boat-to-table seafood fresh from their docks. One of our favorite apps is their famous house smoked fish dip. Here's the recipe which you can make right at home.

local favorite!

INGREDIENTS
(Serves 6-8 people)
2 Lb Smoked Mackeral (Smoke for 2 hours using 3 - 4 ounces of wood. Remove bones and skin)
1/4 Cup Chopped Celery
1/4 Cup Chopped Red Onion
1/4 Cup Chopped Red Bell Pepper
1/2 Lb Softened Cream Cheese
1/2 Cup Mayo
1 Tsp Lemon Juice
1/2 Tsp Old Bay Seasoning

PREPARATION
Soften and whip cream cheese.
Add diced vegetables.
Add remaining ingredients and mix well.
Serve with Tortilla chips or crackers.

You can find Porky's Bayside at 1410 Overseas Hwy (MM 47.5, Bayside) Marathon. 305-289-2065; porkysbaysidebbq.com

Key West's "Sushi Ninja"
AMBROSIA SUSHI & SAKE BAR

Chef/Owner Masa and wife Noriko are making waves at Key West's hip, vintage Santa Maria Hotel. Their edgy sushi restaurant and sake bar is renowned for its authentic, artfully crafted plates, including Masa's premium bluefin tuna creations and other full-flavored dishes like the Spicy Seafood Carpaccio with fresh jalapeño, sweet onion, and Yuzu pepper paste.

Tradition and innovation collide with all kinds of intriguing signature rolls, including the Hamachi Heat - an addictive fusion of snow crab salad, jalapeño, and tempura topped with hamachi, jalapeño slices, Shichimi powder and a side of spicy ponzu. Lots of other Japanese specialties here, too, along with an eclectic selection of artisan sake, fun saketini's, wine, and beer.

Located at 1401 Simonton St. For reservations call 305-293-0304. keywestambrosia.com

SPICY TUNA TARTARE
Ambrosia Sushi Restaurant & Sake Bar, Key West

Chef Masa is renowned for his authentic, artfully crafted plates that raise the bar for inventive Asian fare. This sinful Tuna Tartare tastes as wonderful as it looks.

FOR THE TUNA
(Yield 1 Servings)
8 Oz Sushi Grade Tuna diced into 1/4" cubes
1 Tbl Spicy Korean Miso
1.5 Tsp Japanese Red Pepper Paste
1 Tbl Kimuchi Sauce
2 Tbl Red Tobiko
1 Tsp Minced Jalapeno Pepper
1 Tsp Finely Chopped Scallion
1 Tbl Mayonnaise
Combine tuna and all other ingredients, mix well and chill.

FOR THE GUACAMOLE
1 Hass Avocado
1 Tsp Vinegar
1 Tbl Finely Chopped Jalapeno Pepper
1 Tbl Finely Chopped Onion
1 Tsp Ground Garlic
Mash avocado and combine with all other ingredients, mix well.

FOR THE TOPPING
2 Tbl Shredded Nori
1 Tbl Wasabi Tobiko,
1 Quail Egg Yolk

PREPARATION
Spoon half the tuna mixture on plate, layer with the guacamole and then layer again with the remaining tuna. Top with shredded nori, followed by the wasabi tobiko and finish with the quail egg yolk. Serve with fried spring roll skin.

You can find Ambrosia Sushi Restaurant & Sake Bar at 1401 Simonton St, Key West. 305-293-0304; ambrosiasushi.com

Master Chef John Correa
AWARD-WINNING FOOD AT ITS BEST

John Correa loves, loves, loves food. As Chef/Owner of Key West's award-winning Cafe Sole, he's got his hands on the pots of some of the island's best dishes.

Boat-to-table seafood is the order of the day, and by combining his French mastery of sauces with locally caught fish, Chef Correa creates plates unlike any other restaurant on the island.

Perennial favorites like Tuna Seared In Pistachios with Hoisin garlic sauce with wasabi cream; Grouper Romesco with spicy roasted red pepper/hazelnut sauce; and Correa's signature, award-winning Hog Snapper with roasted red pepper zabaglione. Cafe Sole's extensive menu, which is also peppered with authentic French classics like Duck a' L'Orange, Rack of Lamb with Herbes de Provence, and Lobster Bouillabaisse.

There are lots of intriguing vegetarian options, as well.

The Baked Artichokes stuffed with garlic and crabmeat are especially tasty, and the Virgin Tomato Pasta with a light and yummy sauce made from fresh ripe plum tomato, garlic, Herbes de Provence and white wine is as good as it gets.

FYI: Be sure to leave room for dessert because the Bananas Foster is worth every calorie.

You can find Cafe Sole hidden away at 1029 Southard Street in Old Town Key West. Info: 305-294-0230; cafesole.com.

C'est très bien!

CONCH CARPACCIO
Cafe Sole, Key West

Chef/Owner, John Correa's food is a whoop of earthy, sun-drenched flavor. His seafood-centric menu showcases lots of inventive dishes including this award-winning stand-out.

INGREDIENTS
(Yield 1 Serving)
1 lb Conch meat, #1 grade
1 Tsp Olive Oil
1 Tsp Lime Juice
1 Lime or Lemon
1 Tbl Capers
2 oz Grated Asiago Cheese
Pinch of Red Onion, finely diced
Pinch Red Bell Pepper, finely diced
Salt & Pepper to taste

PREPARATION
Slice conch as thin as possible, see through if you can, half frozen helps. Lay conch out to make a thin layer on a salad plate.

Sprinkle with salt & pepper, cheese, onion, pepper, capers in that order.

Drizzle lime juice and oilve oil over conch.
Do not prepare well in advance.
Garnish with ½ a lime or lemon.

You can find Cafe Sole 1029 Southard Street Key West.
305-293-0230; cafesole.com

Right on the Dock
BISTRO 245, KEY WEST

Bistro 245, a lively open-air restaurant that sits right on the docks of Key West's Opal Resort & Marina is one of my favorite spots to grab a casual bite or sip on a frothy key lime martini.

We always try to snag one of the coveted outside tables overlooking the harbor. Not only is it the perfect place for people-watching, but it also provides a ringside seat for the nightly Sunset Celebration, where live entertainment, music, and a parade of sailboats create the perfect Key West moment.

I have to hand it to Executive Chef Bill Stockton. In a town where chefs turn over faster than flapjacks, Bill has stayed the course for as long as I can remember. He and his culinary team always seem to hit the ball out of the park with island-style creations that will make your head swim.

Top picks for lunch: the Lobster Quesadilla, Spicy Ahi Tuna & Avocado Salad, and the Cuban Classic Sandwich - a signature island concoction made with calypso spiced pork, ham, mojo, swiss and a variety of condiments all pressed together on fresh Cuban bread. Don't leave Key West without trying one of these big babies because chances are; you'll never find one back home.

After 5 pm, Bill and his crew turn up the heat with indulgences like Grilled Chicken Penne with herb garlic cream; Key West Yellowtail Snapper with crabmeat stuffing; Flame Grilled Lemon Garlic Mahi with gruyere mac & cheese; and a terrific 12oz fire seared New York Strip with roasted shiitake mushrooms. Bistro 245 has air-conditioned indoor seating and serves breakfast, lunch, and dinner daily. Find it on the dock behind the Opal Resort & Marina, 245 Front Street in Key West, Fl. Info: 305-292-4320; bistro245.com.

ISLAND GAZPACHO

Bistro 245, Key West

Tucked away on the docks of Opal Resort & Marina, this local favorite overlooks the scenic harbor front and serves the best Sunday Brunch on the island. You can enjoy breakfast, lunch or dinner comfortably indoors or dine casually outside on Sunset Pier which comes alive each evening with entertainment by the famous sunset performers.

INGREDIENTS
(Yield 8 6 oz Servings)
1 Cucumber, peeled & seeded 1/4" dice
1/4 Red Pepper, seeded & 1/4" dice
1/4 Yellow Pepper, seeded & 1/4" dice
1/4 Green Pepper, seeded & 1/4" dice
1/2 Yellow Onion, 1/4" dice
1 Tbl Freshly Chopped Parsley
2 Tbl Fresh Basil, finely cut
2 Tsp Fresh Chopped Dill
½ Cup Celery, finely diced
¾ Cup Italian Dressing (Wishbone Brand)
¾ Cup Tomato Juice
1 - ½ Tsp Fresh Garlic, chopped
1 - ½ Tsp Vietnamese Chili Garlic Sauce
(or any hot sauce of your choice)
1 Tbl Fresh Cilantro, chopped
1 - ½ Cups Fire Roasted Diced Tomatoes & Juice
(Canned will work to save you time)
Salt & Pepper to taste

PREPARATION
Combine all ingredients in stainless steel mixing bowl and mix well. Transfer to storage container. Cover, label, date, and refrigerate. Shelf life is about 3 days.

Find Bistro 245 on the docks of Key West's historic harbor front, 245 Front St, Key West. 305-294-8320; bistro245.com

BURRATA CHEESE
With Balsamic Strawberry Sauce/ Grilled Asparagus & Toasted Red Quinoa
Latitudes At Sunset Key, Key West

Within minutes, the free boat launch at Opal Resort & Marina transports you to this spectacular beachfront restaurant on the island of Sunset Key where you can enjoy outstanding island cuisine like this wonderful Burrata Cheese dish.

(Yield 1 Serving)

INGREDIENTS FOR THE BALSAMIC STRAWBERRY SAUCE

4 Oz Balsamic Vinegar
½ Pint Fresh Strawberries
2 Tbl Agave
2 Tbl Oz Lemon Olive Oil
2 Tbl Lemon Juice

PREPARATION FOR THE SAUCE

Combine all ingredients except olive oil in a sauce pot and reduce to half size in volume. Puree in a blender and pass puree through a fine mesh strainer. When chilled to room temperature whisk in olive oil and refrigerate.

Ingredients for the Quinoa
4 Oz Red Quinoa
6 Oz Water
2 Cups Canola Oil
Kosher Salt, to taste

PREPARATION FOR THE QUINOA

Combine red quinoa and water and bring to a boil. Simmer 3 minutes cover and remove from heat to finish. Remove cooked quinoa from pan onto a parchment paper lined cookie sheet pan. Let cool till you can handle and then break apart so it is singular grain - no clumps. Place in lowest setting of your oven and continue to rub between your hands to remove clumps. When finished, it should be slightly crunchy and resemble singular grains of sand. In a medium large sauce pot heat canola oil to 350°. Pour dried red quinoa into oil and cook till it has a puffed rice texture (1-2 minutes). Strain off oil place quinoa on paper towels to remove excess oil and season to taste

MAIN DISH INGREDIENTS

4 2oz Pieces of Burrata Cheese
20 Spears Pencil Asparagus
1 Pint Fresh Strawberries, washed and quartered
16 Oz Balsamic Strawberry Sauce
4 Tbl Toasted Red Quinoa
2 Tbl Extra Virgin Olive Oil
1 Tbl Thin Sliced Mint
1 Tbl Thin Sliced Basil Leaf
Salt & Pepper to taste

PREPARATION FOR THE BURRATA

Season and grill asparagus, set aside. Brush plate with 3 oz balsamic strawberry sauce. Arrange asparagus on top of balsamic strawberry sauce. With a clean paper towel blot dry burrata cheese and break open to form a cavity. Place burrata on top of asparagus. Toss strawberries with extra virgin olive oil, basil, mint and a pinch of salt and pepper. Place strawberries on top of burrata some will spill out of burrata. Drizzle 1 oz of balsamic strawberry sauce over strawberries and burrata. Sprinkle one level tablespoon of toasted red quinoa over the top. Finish with a few slivers of the mint and basil leaf.

You can board the free boat launch to Sunset Key on the dock behind Opal Resort & Marina at 245 Front St.
Reservations a must! 305-292-5300; sunsetkeycottages.com

It's All About Romance –
LATITUDES RESTAURANT

If you've never lingered over a torch-lit gourmet dinner on the beach of a small private island, maybe it's time to find a new Latitude.

Backdropped by breathtaking views from Sunset Key and just a stone's throw from Key West, Latitudes is the signature restaurant of the Sunset Key Cottages and is one of the most romantic restaurants you'll ever experience.

But romance isn't the only thing on the menu at this celebrated restaurant. The food is just as intoxicating.

Award-winning cuisine and an ever-evolving "work of art" menu take a cue from the ocean views and lean heavily toward seafaring things like Pan-Roasted Rosemary Cobia, Lemon Glazed Yellowtail Snapper, and Pan Roasted Caribbean Lobster Tail.

There are plenty of land-based Island Entrees, as well, including items like Korean barbecued Wagyu Beef Skirt Steak, Grilled Center Cut Beef Tenderloin with onion-bleu cheese-bacon relish Herb-Crusted Mountain, and Mushroom Ragu Linguini.

Whatever mood that you are in, you really can't go wrong with whatever marquees on Latitudes' "can't-miss" menu because everything here is consistently excellent.

This unique "Destination Restaurant" can only be reached by boat. But no worries. The tiny 27-acre island (a favorite of Oprah Winfrey) provides a guest launch that departs from the docks behind Key West's Opal Resort & Marina at 245 Front Street in Key West.

Reservations for Latitudes are an absolute must. The private hideaway is just a quick 10-minute boat ride away, but it's a world apart from anywhere else. Reservations: 855-995-9799; sunsetcottages.com.

Tiki Chic!

SNOOK'S BAYSIDE & GRAND TIKI, KEY LARGO

Key Largo: Keep your eyes peeled when you head north on the Overseas Highway in Key Largo because this bayside "Shangri-La" is easy to miss.

Tucked down a hidden lane under the tropical balm, Snook's Bayside is the kind of place conjured up by the Beach Boys in their iconic hit song, "Kokomo."

A dramatic chandeliered Grand Tiki sets the stage for tropical open-air dining that includes terrific island-inspired fare like Pistachio-Encrusted Yellowtail with mango salsa and chili beurre blanc, Lobster & Shrimp Cakes drizzled with Thai sweet chili, and mango chutney. Try the award-winning Blue Crab-Stuffed Lobster tails finished with béarnaise sauce (Yowza!)

And then there's the view. Oh, that incredibly beautiful view. Fronted by a sprawling 5,000 square foot patio with flickering torches and SOBE-style lounges, Snook's Grand Tiki is backdropped with a gorgeous, unobstructed panorama of the Bay. It also provides a ringside seat to the best nightly Sunset Celebrations in Key Largo, which ceremoniously marks the day's end with a loud blow from Snook's ship's horn.

The celebration continues well after dark with live entertainment and dancing under the palms. What better place to kick back with a fresh whole coconut filled Snook's signature coconut rum punch and enjoy your very own piece of paradise?

Find Snooks Bayside & Grand Tiki at MM 99.8, Southbound Lane behind the Sandal Factory Outlet in Key Largo. Info: 305-453-5004; snooks.com.

YELLOWTAIL SNAPPER
Encrusted with Citrus Zest with Truffle Mashed Potatoes

Snook's Bayside & Grand Tiki, Key Largo

There's no better place to hang your flip flops in the Florida Keys than this hidden waterfront hot spot where spectacular sunsets and casual island fare is always spot on.

INGREDIENTS
(Yield 4 Servings)
4 Fresh Florida Yellowtail Snapper Fillets
4 Large Shrimp
4 Clams In Shell
12 Tbl Butter
1/4 Cup White Wine
1/4 Cup Fish Stock
1 Cup Chopped Artichokes Hearts
6 Tbl Oilive Oil
Zest of 1 Fresh Lime
Zest of 1 Fresh Lemon
Zest of 1 Medium Size Fresh Orange
Salt & Pepper to taste

PREPARATION
Dredge snapper fillets in lemon, orange and lime zest. Season with salt and pepper. Heat skillet to a medium heat with olive oil. Add fillets to skillet and sear for up to 4 minutes per side (Cooking time may vary depending on the thickness of fillets). In a separate sauté pan, add butter, white wine, fish stock, and artichoke hearts. Bring to a simmer. Add shrimp and clams and sauté until clams open and shrimp are pink in color.

TRUFFLE MASHED POTATOES

INGREDIENTS
2 Lbs Potatoes
1 Cup Light Cream
6 Tbl Butter
1 Tbl Chopped Garlic
2 Tbl Fine Truffle Oil
Salt & pepper to Taste

PREPARATION
Place potatoes into a large saucepan and cover with water. Bring to a boil over high heat. Cook until fork tender, about 25 minutes. Drain the potatoes and return to a low heat for 2 to 3 minutes to dry up any excess water. In a separate small saucepan, warm the cream and butter over medium heat until it melts together. Using a masher, mash the potatoes in the saucepan. Add the garlic, cream, butter, salt and pepper and mix well. Stir in fine truffle oil.

FOR SALAD
Combine fresh watercress with cherry tomatoes and freshly chopped fennel and toss with your favorite vinaigrette.

You can find Snook's Bayside at MM 99.9 Bayside, Key Largo
305-453-5004; snooks.com

Something To Crow About

THE BUZZARD'S ROOST, KEY LARGO

1f you're looking for a terrific waterfront restaurant that's far from the madding crowds, tell Siri to take you to "The Buzzard's Roost" in Key Largo.

Situated dockside at the Garden Cove Marina, this cozy spot may be off the beaten track, but the food is all that and a bag of chips.

You'll find loads of fresh fish dishes and local seafood, as well as belly-buster sandwiches, big, juicy chargrilled Black Angus burgers, jumbo chicken wings, and a whole lot more.

Whatever you do, do not, we repeat, do not pass up the Smoked Fish Dip, Lobster Reuben, or Corny Blue Crabakes with New Orleans-style remoulade sauce. All are fabulous and worthy Blue Ribbon winners.

Big plates run the gamut from Shrimp Scampi, Seafood Combo Platter, and Fried Shrimp to Chicken Marsala, certified Black Angus Steaks, and slow-roasted BBQ Baby Back Ribs.

Soar on in for Happy Hour at the inside bar Monday through Friday from 4 - 6 pm or at the outside tiki bar on Friday nights from 4-7 pm. Buzzard's Roost has terrific live music.

FYI: The Sunday Brunch is just as fabulous and includes complimentary mimosas!

Discover this hidden gem just before the entrance of Card Sound Road at 21 Garden Cove Drive, MM 106.5, Oceanside in Key Largo. Info: 305-453-3746; buzzardsroostkeylargo.com.

Rest assured — you won't find a better waterfront spot to roost!

CHIPOTLE GLAZED MAHI-MAHI
with Fresh Mango & Strawberry Salsa
The Buzzard's Roost, Key Largo

Named for Key Largo's high ground, called "Wachula," which mean's "buzzard's roost" in the native Seminole language, this intimate Keys hideaway overlooking Garden Cove Marina has some of the best food around. The Sunday Brunch here is also just as outstanding.

INGREDIENTS FOR FISH
(Yield 2 Servings)
2 - 8 Oz Mahi-Mahi Fillets
1 Tbl Chipotle/Roasted Garlic Seasoning (available in grocery stores)
½ Cup Chipotle Glaze (available in grocery stores)
1/2 Tbl Extra Virgin Olive Oil
Fruit Salsa (recipe follows)

INGREDIENTS FOR SALSA
(Yield 1-½ Cups)
1 Mango, cubed
3-4 Strawberries, diced
1 Tbl Red Onion, finely chopped
1 Tbl Cilantro, finely chopped
2 Tbl Sugar
½ Fresh Jalapeño, seeded and minced

PREPARATION FOR SALSA
Add the diced strawberries to a bowl and cover with sugar. Mix together and let stand for 30 minutes. Add remaining ingredients and mix thoroughly. Add salt and pepper to taste.

PREPARATION FOR FISH
Heat a non-stick skillet with 1/2 Tbl olive oil over medium-high heat. Season fillets with chipotle/roasted garlic seasoning and add to skillet when oil begins to smoke. Reduce heat and turn fish after 3 minutes; cook until flakey. Drizzle 1 Tbl of the chipotle glaze on fish while in pan to warm up. Remove fish and serve over your favorite beans and rice recipe. Top fish with salsa and drizzle remaining chipotle sauce around plate and on top of plated fish.

You can find The Buzzard's Roost at 21 Garden Cove Dr, just off the Overseas Hwy at Card Sound Road in Key Largo. 305-453-3746; buzzardsroostkeylargo.com

Fresh Off the Boat –
The Fish House Restaurant & Seafood Market, Key Largo

Ask any local where to eat in Key Largo and dollars to donuts; the Fish House will be at the top of the list.

Featured on the "Food Network," The Fish House has been a Key Largo landmark for over 35 years. Owners Doug Prew and CJ Berwick opened the rough-hewn roadside restaurant in 1987, just as the Conch Republic was being born.

"In the late 1980s, we were at the tail end of the Wild West here in the Keys," Doug once recalled. "We used to play touch football on US 1. We could play half a game of football before seeing a car".

But those early days did not deter Doug and CJ. Even back then, they knew that the key to terrific seafood lies in its freshness, so they made "fresh off the boat" fish their trademark. "From our fishermen to you!" became their official slogan, but more than that, it became their mission and mantra for the decades that followed.

Today, local fisherman still bring their daily catches — 3,000 to 4,000 pounds a week to the back door of The Fish House, where it's filleted on premises.

Topping the menu are homemade chowder, smoked fish dip, and "Today's Catch Specialty Preparations," which include the award-winning Matecumbe Style (topped with fresh tomatoes, shallots, fresh basil, capers, olive oil, and lemon, then baked).

Many of the fish dishes here are prepared "island style," but you can also get fried seafood platters, whole yellowtail snapper, king crab, Florida lobster, and more.

And even though it's a "Fish House," you can still enjoy Black Angus steak, baby back ribs, grilled chicken, and lots of pasta.

This landmark eatery is open daily from 11am - 10pm. Find it at 102401 Overseas Hwy (MM 102.4 Oceanside) in Key Largo. Info: 305-451-4665; fishhouse.com.

FISH MATECUMBE
The Fish House, Key Largo

Inspired by a beloved dish at The Fish House in Key Largo, this house specialty is a favorite of Food Network Celebrity Chefs, Bobby Flay and Guy Fieri. A simple approach using fresh locally caught fish topped with a salsa made from lemon, tomatoes, onions and capers is a real winner.

INGREDIENTS
(Yield 8 Servings)
- 8 Fish Fillets of your choice
- 5 Tomatoes, chopped
- 1/2 Spanish Onion, chopped
- 8 Oz Jar of Capers, drained
- 1 Cup Extra Virgin Olive Oil
- 1/4 Chopped Fresh Basil
- 2 Fresh Lemons, juiced
- 5 Shallots, chopped
- 1-1/2 Tsp Each Salt & Pepper

PREPARATION
Add the olive oil, capers, basil, shallots, tomatoes, lemon juice, onions, 1-1/2 teaspoons salt and 1 1/2 teaspoons pepper to a medium bowl and stir to thoroughly combine. Refrigerate until ready to use, at least 1 hour and up to overnight. Position an oven rack at least 4 inches but no more than 6 inches from the broiler and preheat the broiler. Place the fish fillets on a baking sheet and season with salt and pepper. Place under the broiler and cook until done on one side; watch carefully, as it may only take a couple minutes depending on the thickness of your fillets and the proximity to the broiler. Remove from the broiler and turn each fillet over. Top each fillet with about 1/2 cup of the sauce. Return to the broiler and cook until the fish is done on the other side and fully cooked through in the middle. If you are unsure about doneness, cut into the center of the fillets; the fish should be opaque (you can cover up the cut with the sauce).

You can find the award-winning Fish House Restaurant & Seafood Market at MM 102.4 Oceanside in Key Largo. 305-451-4665; fishhouse.com

RED STRIPE BRAISED SHORT RIBS
WITH SWEET POTATO PUREE
M.E.A.T, Islamorada

Sweet, salty and a little sour, award-winning Chef George Patti's signature short rib recipe is pure comfort food that is is just so mmm, mmm, good!

INGREDIENTS
(Yield 4 Servings)
Boneless Beef Short Ribs
(7 oz. per person)
2 Onions Coarsely Diced
2 Carrots Coarsely Diced
5 Cloves Garlic
6 Sprigs Thyme
1/2 Tsp. Chili Flakes
2 Cans Chicken Stock
(14 oz)
2 Bay Leaves
5 Peppercorns
1/4 Cup Jerk Seasoning
1 Tsp. Allspice
5 Cans Red Stripe Beer
1 Cup Dale Steak Seasoning (or soy sauce)

RIB PREPARATION
Preheat oven to 350°. Mix together all dry ingredients, chicken stock and only three bottles of the Red Stripe Beer. Place mixture in large braising pan. Set aside. In a separate skillet, sear ribs over high heat, four or five at a time, with olive oil seasoned with kosher salt. Remove from stove and add seared short ribs to braising pan. Cover with foil and bake for 1-1/2 hours. In the meantime, remove one bottle of Red Stripe Beer from fridge, open and enjoy. After 1-1/2 hours, turn ribs and bake an additional 1-1/2 hours. Return to fridge and grab another bottle of Red Stripe. Open and imbibe. Ribs should be fork tender when finished and you should be smiling.

FOR SWEET POTATO PUREE
4 Med. Sweet Potatoes - Peeled
6 Tbl Unsalted Butter
1 Tsp Five Spice
3 Tbl Heavy Cream

PREPARATION
Boil sweet potatoes with salt until fork tender. Drain and let dry. Place all ingredients in blender and blend until smooth. If needed, add a little more cream until desired consistency.

Season with salt. Enjoy!

You can find M.E.A.T. Eatery and Taproom at 88005 Overseas Hwy, Islamorada 305-852-3833; meateatery.com

PINA COLADA SHRIMP
With Pineapple Chipotle Dipping Sauce
Olive Morada, Islamorada

The key to this tasty tropical dish is the pairing of the flavored balsamic vinegars with the infused chipotle olive oil. You can find these, along with all kinds of other fine imported olive oils, specialty oils and balsamic vinegars, at Olive Morada in Islamorada.

FOR THE DIPPING SAUCE
3 Oz Olive Morada's Pineapple Balsamic Vinegar
3 Oz Olive Morada's Infused Chipotle Olive Oil
4 Oz Mayonnaise (may substitute sour cream or Greek yogurt)
1/2 Tbl Sugar
Emulsify all ingredients together, and chill

FOR THE SHRIMP
(Yield 4 Servings)
1.5 Lb. or 13-15 Shrimp (peeled and deveined, do not remove the tails)
8 oz. Rice Flour
1/4 Cup Shredded Coconut
1/2 Cup Olive Morada's Coconut Balsamic Vinegar
1/4 Cup Olive Morada's Pineapple Balsamic Vinegar
1/2 Cup sparkling water (must be cold)
4 Tbl Corn Starch for dusting
Himalayan Pink Sea Salt and Ground Black Pepper, to taste
Vegetable Oil for frying

PREPARATION
Put vegetable oil in a heavy bottom pan or fryer and heat 375°. Mix together all ingredients except for corn starch and shrimp, and whisk until smooth.

Yowza!

Coat shrimp with corn starch and dip shrimp in batter until completely coated. Fry in oil for 3-5 minutes or until golden brown. Serve Pina Colada Shrimp with dipping sauce, and enjoy!

You'll be amazed at how many delicious possibilities you can whip up in your kitchen using Olive Morada's line of fine imported olive oils, specialty oils and balsamic vinegars.

Thanks to Catherine in Long Grove for this Original Recipe

For a complete selection of vinegars and olive oils, visit Olive Morada, 82245 Overseas Hwy Islamorada. 305-735-4375; olivemorada.com

BACON WRAPPED LOVE

Green Turtle Inn, Florida Keys

When celebrity chef Guy Fieri visited Islamorada's iconic Green Turtle Inn, he was so blown away with the restaurant's signature meatloaf recipe that he featured it on the Food Network's hit show, "Diners, Drive-ins and Dives." Here's your chance to make it right at home.

INGREDIENTS FOR MEATLOAF

(Yield 6 - 8 Servings)
5 Lbs 80% Beef/20% Pork Ground Meat Blend
1-1/4 Cups Panko Breadcrumbs
1/2 Cup Milk
1/2 Cup Small-Diced Green Bell Pepper
1/2 Cup Small-Diced Red Bell Pepper
1/2 Cup Small-Diced Sweet Onion
1/4 Cup Minced Garlic
1/4 Cup Minced Mixed Fresh Parsley and Chives
1/4 Cup Worcestershire Sauce
2 Tbl Ground Coriander
2 Tbl Onion Powder
1 Tbl Kosher Salt
1/2 Tbl Ground Black Pepper
1/2 Tbl Ground White Pepper
2 Eggs
Clarified Butter, for searing
1 Quart Sliced Crimini Mushrooms
1/2 Cup Bistro Sauce, recipe follows
16 Strips Bacon
2 Cups Ketchup

INGREDIENTS FOR BISTRO SAUCE

3 Cups Canned Tomato Fillets
1/8 Cup Water
2 Cups Coca-Cola
1/2 Cup Soy Sauce
1/2 Cup Worcestershire Sauce
1/8 Cup Garlic Powder
1/8 Cup Ground black Pepper
1/6 Cup Sugar
1/6 Cup Italian Seasoning
1/8 Cup Kosher Salt
1 Tbs Sriracha
1/2 Lb Raisins

PREPARATION FOR MEATLOAF

Preheat the oven to 375°
Combine the meat, panko, milk, bell peppers, onion, garlic, herbs, Worcestershire sauce, coriander, onion powder, salt, black pepper, white pepper and eggs in a large mixing bowl. By hand, fold all the ingredients together until thoroughly mixed. Remove a small amount of the mixture and sear it in clarified butter in a skillet over medium heat until cooked through, 4 to 5 minutes, to test for flavor and consistency. The meat may appear under-seasoned; this is okay.

In a separate mixing bowl, combine the mushrooms and Bistro Sauce and mix thoroughly.

Place the mushrooms in a fine-mesh sieve set over a bowl and let the excess sauce drain off and collect in a bowl; reserve for the glaze.

Line a sheet pan with the bacon in a crisscross weave pattern. Put approximately half the meatloaf mix into the pan and spread out evenly. Make a vein of mushrooms that runs down the entire center of the pan. Take the rest of the meatloaf mix and cover the mushrooms in an even layer. Fold the bacon over the meatloaf. Flip the meatloaf over onto a lined sheet pan.

Bake the meatloaf for 20 minutes. Lower the oven temperature to 350°. Cover the meatloaf with foil and continue baking until the internal temperature reaches 165 degrees F, about 20 additional minutes. Combine the reserved Bistro Sauce with the ketchup and refrigerate until ready to serve. Top the meatloaf with the sauce before serving.

You can find the iconic Green Turtle Inn at 81219 Overseas Hwy, Islamorada
305-664-2006; greenturtleinn.com

Legendary Food & a Storied Past
ZIGGIE & MAD DOG'S, ISLAMORADA

The Keys' storied past is ripe with colorful tales and locations worthy of a Mickey Spillane novel. Islamorada's highly acclaimed Ziggie & Mad Dog's is no exception.

Initially built in the 1930s as an outbuilding on a local pineapple plantation, the property first grabbed headlines in 1948 when the Miami Herald reported stories of police shootouts with gamblers and shady characters referred to as "The new Capone gang."

Chicago Mob Boss, Al Capone, was rumored to be involved in the high-stakes card games and casino action held in the back building before it morphed into a small restaurant in the 1950s.

Then in 1962, Sigmund "Ziggie" Stocki, an alleged drifter, gambler, and casino maitre d' opened "Ziggie The Conch Restaurant."

With its Formica-topped tables, paper placemats, and lime green walls, Ziggie's was a real no-frills joint but its "New World Fusion Cuisine," which combined fresh local seafood with Caribbean-Asian recipes, was way ahead of its time.

Soon, Ziggie's became the hottest ticket in town, attracting celebrities, including the legendary actor Paul Newman.

In the thirty years of operation, "Ziggie The Conch" was world-renowned as one of the most exceptional dining experiences in the Florida Keys, and his culinary influence is still ev-ident today in many of the Keys' best restaurants.

In 2005, the late Jim "Mad Dog" Mandich, a former tight end for the Miami Dolphins' un-defeated 1972 Super Bowl team, along with business partner, Randy Kassewitz, resurrected the popular Keys icon to its old glory days.

Today, the legend lives on, and you can still rub elbows with an eclectic crowd of famous celebrities, sports stars, and notorious fishing captains who glam to this popular hot spot for orchid-garnished cocktails, fine wines, and outstanding steaks, chops, and seafood.

Find it at MM 83, Bayside in Islamorada. Open nightly at 5:30 pm. Info: 305-664-3391; ziggieandmaddogs.com.

HONEY GRILLED CHICKEN & MASHED SWEET POTATO

Ziggie & Mad Dog's, Islamorada

Executive Chef John Strain reached back to his southern roots for this refined yet simple chicken dish. While growing up in Georgia, John and his father would often stop before dawn to get homemade fried chicken and biscuits on their way to hunt dove and quail. The homemade food from an old stone building in Cave Spring became one of his fondest food memories. Something about that comforting, well-seasoned chicken with the sweet and spicy combination of honey and hot sauce, enjoyed with friends and family, stuck with him. Today, that lasting memory is now a top requested dish at Islamorada's acclaimed Ziggie & Mad Dog's Restaurant. We hope you enjoy it as much as we do.

INGREDIENTS
(Yield 2 Servings)
2 8 Oz all natural organic, skin-on airline chicken breasts
4 Tbl Honey
2 Tbl Whole Grain Mustard
2 Tbl Hot Sauce
2 Tbl Salted Butter
2 Jumbo sweet potatoes, peeled, boiled and mashed

PREPARATION
Season the chicken with Kosher salt and cracked black pepper. Grill on high heat, skin down for two to three minutes until skin begins to crisp. Place on baking sheet, skin up and finish in a 400° oven for approximately 15 minutes or until internal temp reaches 160°.

In the meantime, combine honey, mustard, and hot sauce in a small saucepan and cook on medium for about two minutes; add mashed sweet potatoes, reduce heat, whip in butter.

TO SERVE
Arrange the chicken around the sweet mash, drizzle the chicken with the honey reduction and finish by spooning on the cooking liquid from the baking sheet. Reserve the remaining reduction to be served on the side for dipping.

You can find Ziggie & Mad Dog's at MM 83, Bayside in Islamorada 305-664-3391; ziggieandmaddogs.com.

Life's A Beach!
Lazy Days In Islamorada

Nothing says "Lazy Days in the Keys" more than wiggling your toes in the sand, Key Lime Mojito in hand, and dining on boat-to-table seafood: all that backdropped with a spectacular stretch of Atlantic as far as your eyes can see.

Life sure feels good at Islamorada's award-winning Lazy Day's Restaurant, which is why it's one of the Upper Keys' most popular hangs.

"Keys-style" cooking is the specialty here, and loyal customers clamor in for signature preparations of local seafood.

If you're looking for a great fish sandwich, the one served here is a hands-down winner. You can get it all the usual ways: fried, grilled, blackened, sautéed, or ranchero style. But what will knock your socks off is the coconut fried version. No one in the Keys can touch it.

The crab cakes are also exceptional — nice and meaty with key lime butter and béarnaise sauce.

For dinner, the kitchen turns up the heat with entree specials like the fabulous Seafood Fra Diavlo — a half lobster, whole mussels, clams, shrimp, and local shrimp sautéed with peppers, mushrooms, onions, and tomatoes in a spicy marinara sauce.

The Jumbo Stuffed Shrimp, baked with fresh crabmeat stuffing and topped with béarnaise sauce and key lime butter, is also a local favorite.

But what rocks the house is the signature Lazy Days Fish — a fresh fillet rolled in Japanese bread crumbs, sautéed and topped with fresh diced tomatoes, scallions, shredded parmesan cheese, and key lime butter.

If you're looking for something "meatier," opt for the Choice hand-cut New York Strip, char-grilled Filet, Chicken Piccata, or any of the tasty pasta dishes.

Lazy Days sits right on the beach oceanside at MM 79.9. You can eat inside, right on the beach, or alfresco on the restaurant's big wrap-around porch.

Open daily at 11 am for lunch and dinner. Info: 305-664-5256; lazydaysislamorada.com.

FISH WITH KEY LIME BUTTER SAUCE

Lazy Days Restaurant, Islamorada

Lazy Days Restaurant is a place where you can kick up your feet and enjoy award-winning Keys-style dishes in a spectacular oceanfront setting. This lovely dish is one of the most popular on the menu. Serve it with garlic mashed potatoes and a nice Pinot Grigio for a dinner that's made to impress!

INGREDIENTS
(Yield 4 Servings)
2 Lbs Fish Fillets, like Yellowtail Snapper or other white fish
1 Tbl Key Lime Juice
2 Cups Panko Breadcrumbs
2 Tbs Fresh Parsley, chopped
1 Cup Scallion, chopped
1 Cup Tomato, chopped
2 Large Eggs
1/2 Tsp Garlic powder
3 Tsp Cornstarch
1 Cup Flour
1/8 Tsp White Pepper, fresh ground
1/4 Lb Butter
1/2 Cup Parmesan Cheese, grated
1/4 Cup Dry White Wine
1 - 3/16 Cup Water

PREPARATION:

Place the water, wine and key lime juice in a large saucepan over a high heat and reduce by half, about 5 minutes. Add the garlic power. Add pepper to taste. Cut the butter into pats about the size of 1 tablespoon. Reduce the heat to low. Add one pat butter and whisk until the butter is incorporated. Add another pat and continue until all of the butter is used. Mix the water and cornstarch together and add to the sauce. Raise the heat to medium and stir until the sauce thickens and a few bubbles appear. Set aside while the fish cooks.

Mix the eggs and water together in a small bowl (whisk vigorously, until combined). Place the flour on a plate and dip the fish fillets into flour, coating both sides. Dip the fish into the egg wash. Place the bread crumbs on a second plate and coat the fish with bread crumbs, making sure both sides are coated. Heat 4 tablespoons of the Key lime butter sauce over medium-high heat in a skillet large enough to hold the fish in one layer. Add the fish and sauté for 4 minutes until golden. Use a little olive oil for sautéing, if necessary. Turn the fish and sauté for 4 minutes for 1 inch-thick fillets. Sauté 2 minutes longer for thicker fish or 2 minutes less for thinner fish. The fish is cooked when the flesh is opaque, not translucent. Place the fish on 4 dinner plates. Spoon the sauce over each piece and sprinkle with the tomatoes, scallions, parmesan cheese and parsley.

You can find Lazy Days right on the beach at 79867 Overseas Hwy (MM 79. Oceanside) in Islamorada. 305-664-5256; lazydaysislamorada.com.

Puttin On The Dog!
CIAO HOUND ITALIAN KITCHEN & BAR, ISLAMORADA

Executive Chef Eduardo Rodrigues likes to keep things simple at Islamorada's Ciao Hound Italian Kitchen & Bar: from his brick oven flatbreads, pastas and al forno parmigiana, to his grilled Mahi-Mahi Puttanesca, Sweet Pan-Seared Florida Shrimp and garlic-rosemary basted Sirloin Steak.

"Simple ingredients bring out the flavor," says Rodrigues, who expertly pairs classic Italian comfort foods and authentic Tuscan flavors with locally-sourced ingredients.

And boy, he's not kidding.

Rodrigues' handcrafted tomato sauce starts with San Marzano tomatoes imported directly from Italy, and it's the foundation of many of his beautiful creations.

Some of our favorites include signature dishes like the Chicken Saltimbocca - pan-fried prosciutto and tender, sage-wrapped chicken medallions with marsala wine sauce, mushrooms and mozzarella, as well as the Linguini Vongole - sweet tender clams, garlic, lemon, and a touch of white wine, Pomodoro red or white sauce.

But what puts the "Hound" in Ciao Hound is the outdoor Fido-friendly dining area. Where leashed dogs can dine on fine canine cuisine like the "Hen House Chicken Strips" — grilled and sliced chicken breast tossed with spinach and penne pasta; the "Half Pounder" - 8 ounces of ground beef served over cubed polenta, and the "Happy Puppy" — a 6 ounce fire-seared steak served with cannelloni beans.

And as if that's not enough, Ciao Hound puts on the dog during its daily 5 - 6 pm "Yappy Hour" with daily specials for both you and your pup.

Dinner served nightly from 5 - 10pm. Full bar with classic cocktails and nearly a dozen Italian-inspired cocktails. FYI: The Loaded Bloody Mary, served with prosciutto-wrapped shrimp and a chicken wing, is the bomb!

You can find Ciao Hound Italian Kitchen & Bar at 84001 Overseas Highway (MM 84, Oceanside) in Islamorada. Info: 305-664-5300; ciaohound84.com.

FRUTTI DI MARE
Ciao Hound Italian Kitchen & Bar, Islamorada

One of Islamorada's newest "people and pet friendly" eateries is fast tracked to becoming an Upper Keys favorite. With authentic Tuscan flavors, Keys-sourced ingredients and Rat Pack-era tunes, Ciao Hound is turning traditional Italian dining on its head. Here's the recipe for a signature dish you can make right at home.

INGREDIENTS
(Yield Two Servings)
7 Oz Linguini Pasta
4 Fresh Mussels
4 Fresh Clams
4 Shrimp, 16/20
4 Oz Calamari Rings
4 Oz White Wine
1 Oz Fresh Garlic, chopped
2 Oz Marinara Sauce
1/2 C torn fresh Basil
1 Oz Corn Oil
Salt and Pepper to taste
Garlic Bread.

PREPARATION
Cook pasta as directed. Set aside. Heat a sauté pan. Add olive oil and sauté garlic until lightly golden and aromatic. Deglaze the pan with white wine. Add clams, mussels and marinara sauce. Cover and simmer until the clams and mussels open up. Add the shrimp and calamari. Continue to cook for 1 minute. Add the reheated pasta & basil and lightly toss with the sauce until coated. Check seasoning and serve in large pasta bowl.

You can find Ciao Hound Kitchen & Bar, MM84 Oceanside at the Postcard Inn Islamorada 305-664-5300; ciaohound84.com

The People Have Spoken
KEY COLONY INN, KEY COLONY BEACH

There's a reason people keep going back to the Key Colony Inn night after night.

Located right next to the Key Colony Beach Golf Course, this local institution feels more like a private, old-time country club than it does a family restaurant.

Consistently voted "Best Overall Restaurant In Marathon" by the Florida Keys People's Choice Awards, the Key Colony Inn draws a dedicated local crowd who come here regularly for the lively bar scene and great Italian, seafood and continental specialties.

The menu here is amazingly extensive and varied. So much so that you'll be hard-pressed to choose what to have.

The Seafood Italiano — shrimp and scallops with mushrooms sautéed in garlic butter with a hint of marinara sauce over a bed of linguini and the Chicken Romano — chicken breast sautéed in lemon, butter, and sherry topped with artichokes and crabmeat, both get a definite two thumbs up.

For big appetites, the Fisherman's Platter, piled high with delicious fresh fish, conch, shrimp, scallops, and a half lobster, can be sautéed or fried. It's a seafood lover's dream and perfect for sharing.

There are also quite a few veal dishes that are outrageously good, as well. Our favorite: the Veal Oscar baked with white wine, then topped with asparagus and shrimp with a silky smooth béarnaise sauce.

Steak lovers have plenty to choose from, too: New York Strip, Filet Mignon, Filet Tournedos, a 12 oz. Angus Au Poivre, and more. The weekend Prime Rib special is also top drawer. Plump and juicy, it always draws big crowds on Friday, Saturday, and Sunday nights.

And speaking of weekends, in-season, the KC Inn also puts out a terrific Sunday Brunch from 11 am – 2 pm. This vast, all-you-can-eat buffet is chock full of both breakfast and lunch selections, $2.00 Bloody Mary's, and decadent homemade desserts.

The Key Colony Inn is located just off the Overseas Hwy on Key Colony Beach, MM54, oceanside in Marathon. Take your first right after coming over the Causeway. The restaurant will be just on your right at 700 W Ocean Drive. Open daily at 11 am, for lunch and dinner. Info: 305-743-0100; kcinn.com.

SCALLOPS NEW BRUNSWICK

Key Colony Inn, Key Colony Beach

The menu at this family owned award-winning restaurant has a huge selection of seafood but it's the fresh seared sea scallops simmered in white wine and heavy cream that really knock the ball out of the park.

INGREDIENTS
(Yield 1 Serving)
10 oz. Fresh Sea Scallops (10/20)
1 Tsp Minced Garlic
1 Tbl Butter
1 Tbl Lemon Juice
Pinch of Crushed Black Pepper
Pinch Fresh Rosemary
1 Tbl Brandy
1 oz White Wine
1 Tbl Chopped Cooked Bacon
1 Tbl Finely Chopped Parsley
1 Lemon Wedge

PREPARATION
Heat pan until hot. Sear scallops in butter and garlic until slightly brown. Add pinch of pepper, lemon juice and brandy. Reduce heat to medium. Add white wine and simmer one minute. Add bits of bacon and rosemary. Add heavy cream and continue to simmer until sauce thickens. Garnish with a sprig of fresh rosemary, finely chopped parsley and lemon.

CHEF'S TIP
Make sure your pan is very, very hot before adding the scallops. For a thicker sauce add a small amount of roux (equal amounts of melted butter and flour cooked until golden brown).

You can find Key Colony in at 700 West Ocean Drive, Key Colony Beach, oceanside at MM 53.5 in Marathon. 305-743-0100; kcinn.com

Pete The Greek
The Guy Behind 7 Mile Grill

Pull up a chair at Marathon's historic 7 Mile Grill and chances are you'll be greeted by the strikingly handsome Pete "The Greek" Chekimoglou.

But don't let those good looks and easy manner fool you. Like many small restaurateurs, "The Greek" works non-stop from morning 'til night. In fact, if you didn't know better, you'd think the guy never sleeps because he's almost always there even though his rustic dockside eatery is open seven days a week for breakfast, lunch, and dinner.

Not that Pete's omnipresence is the only reason the 7 Mile Grill is so popular.

It's all about the food which is just sooo damn good.

You'll find lots of terrific fresh seafood, pasta, burgers, and light bites here, but it's Pete's authentic Greek specialties that get our tongues wagging.

For starters, order the Spanakopita (spinach pie) or Tirokafteri (spicy feta dip). Pete's old-world recipes won't disappoint, and you'll be tempted to get a couple of extra orders to go.

It's the hand-held Gyros that we can't ever seem to pass up. Served on fresh pita bread and over-stuffed with sliced Gyro meat, lettuce, tomato, onion, and house-made Tzatziki (yogurt) sauce; they are heavenly and will make you feel like you were eating at a genuine Greek Taverna.

The Souvlaki, which you can get with chicken or pork, is just as yummy and also comes wrapped in pita with LTO and Tzatziki.

The 7 Mile Grill certainly isn't fancy, but if it's excellent food you're looking for in a casual dockside Keys setting.

7 Mile Grill is one place you need to check out! Find it at 1240 Overseas Hwy, in Marathon. Info: 305-743-4481; 7-Mile-Grill.com.

SHRIMP SAGANAKI
7 Mile Grill, Marathon

The 7 Mile Grill is the best spot in the Keys for authentic Greek specialties. You'll never believe that this yummy dish only takes about 15 minutes to prepare and ten minutes to cook. It is just so damn good!

INGREDIENTS
(Yield 2 Servings)
Extra Virgin Olive Oil
1Lb Shrimp, peeled and deveined
1 Small or 1/2 White Onion, diced
1 Large Tomato, diced
6 oz Feta Cheese, crumbled
2 Oz Ouzo
Oregano to your liking
Salt & Pepper

PREPARATION
Line olive oil on bottom of pan, add onion salt & pepper. Sauté until onions are soft and translucent. Add shrimp and tomato and cook for 2-3 minutes. Turn shrimp, add the feta and sprinkle with oregano. Cook for further 2-3 minutes then pour 2 ounces of Ouzo over shrimp. Light and quickly flambé to burn off alcohol.

Serve with garlic bread, essential to mop up the delicious sauce.

You can find the 7 Mile Grill at MM 47.5, Gulfside in Marathon
305-743-4481; SevenMileGrill.com

A Last Little Piece of Old Key West
SCHOONER WHARF BAR & GRILL

It was in November 1984 when Paul and Evalena Worthington quietly sailed into the Key West Bight on their classic 1926 Alden Schooner Defiance. Anchored by sea-battered shrimp boats and buffered by wooden shanties selling nautical wares, the rough and ramshackle harbor front was a sight to behold.

Entrepreneurs that they were, the seafaring

couple immediately got to work on establishing the largest marine fuel dealership south of Miami. They also set their sights on an even more significant challenge: transforming the Key West Bight into a thriving Historic Seaport District. Their sheer resolve and hard work paid off. Schooner Wharf is now home to the largest working fleet of Schooners on the East coast.

But that's only the back story.

In 1986 - just a short two years after they arrived in Key West - they also opened the now-infamous Schooner Wharf Bar. Originally located aboard the Brigantine Diamonte, it became a floating "living room" for the colorful waterfront community.

Eventually, the Worthington's moved their boat bar ashore where a diving board served as the bar top, a filing cabinet housed the top-shelf liquor, and local marine salvage became "eclectic" decor.

Today, this last little piece of old Key West just keeps getting better with time. The funky open-air bar – located on the site of the old Singleton Shrimp factory – is a beacon for both locals and visitors.

But don't be fooled by the looks of this rustic dockside "dive."

The food here may not be fancy, but it's sure damn good.

Fresh stone crab claws, peel-and-eat shrimp, fresh-shucked oysters, and, of course, conch chowder and fritters, headline the no-frills menu.

You can also get Schooner Wings with a choice of sauces, big chargrilled burgers, grilled or blackened fish sandwiches, and lots of other handhelds, as well as several hearty Galley Plates.

Good food, exceptional live local entertainment, and a colorful cast of customers keep this last little piece of old Key West one of the island's coolest hangs.

You can find SWBG at 202 William Street on the docks of the historic Key West Harbor Front in Old Town Key West. Info: 305-292-9520; schoonerwharf.com

FILET MIGNON, ISLAND STYLE

Schooner Wharf Bar, Key West

An island institution since 1984, this ramshackle open-air bar is a slice of "Old Key West" and is "as funky as a pair of well-worn flip flops." The menu here pretty much mirrors the same fare served at all the other local dives but with one exception: Schooner Wharf does it a helluva lot better. The raw bar and seafood is impeccably fresh but it's this Filet Mignon recipe that really takes the cake!

INGREDIENTS
(Yield 4 Servings)
4 Prime Filet Mignon
1 Pint Jack Daniels
1 Pint Courvoisier
1 Pint Vodka
2 Tsp Bitters
2 Tsp Fresh Lemond Rind
1 Qt Perrier

PREPARATION:
With the exception of the steaks, combine all ingredients and mix thoroughly. Set aside. Cook filets over high heat for 4 minutes. Flip steaks and continuing cooking for another 4 minutes. Remove from heat and let meat rest for about 10 minutes to retain the juices. Quickly dip the filets into the liquid mixture. Remove and pat dry. Cut filet into hearty chunks. Throw to the dogs and drink the "gravy."

You can find the historic Schooner Wharf Bar at
202 William St, Key West. 305-392-9520; schoonerwharf.com

HONEY CITRUS GLAZED SALMON

Lighthouse Grill, Marathon

Framed by a towering lighthouse, this casual bay front restaurant serves up an eclectic menu of fresh seafood creations and local favorites. If you're a fan of salmon, this honey citrus glazed preparation may be right up your alley.

INGREDIENTS
(Yield 2 Servings)
2 - 8 Oz Fresh Organic Salmon Filet
2 Tbl Extra Virgin Olive Oil
Kosher Salt & Black Pepper to taste
1 Lemon, quartered
Fresh Lotus Root, julienned

HONEY CITRUS GLAZE
6 Oz Apple Blossom Honey
1.5 Oz Fresh Ginger, minced
1 Orange, juiced
1 Fresh Lime, juiced
Zest of 1 Lime
Combine all ingredients and set aside.

PREPARATION
Rinse salmon fillets well and pat dry. Brush with Honey Citrus Glaze. Squeeze a 1/4 lemon over fillets. Season with Kosher salt and pepper. Heat a heavy skillet over medium heat. When the skillet is hot, add enough olive oil to coat bottom. Add the salmon to the hot pan and sear undisturbed for 3 minutes until light golden brown. Use a spatula to turn fish over and cook another 3 minutes until the fish is gold, crispy and just barely opaque all the way through. (Cooking time may vary depending on the thickness of the fillet. You can see the degree of doneness by looking at sides of fillet). While the fish is cooking, fry the julienned lotus root until crispy and season with salt and pepper.

Place cooked salmon on platter and garnish with flash fried lotus root and lemon wedge.

You can find Lighthouse Grill located at the Hyatt Faro Blanco Resort & Yacht Club, MM 48.5 Gulfside in Marathon. 305-434-9047; faroblancoresort.com

CILANTRO-SEARED SWORDFISH
with Roasted Red Beet and Kale and Caramelized Shallot Beurre Blanc

Tavern N' Town, Key West

With a "Tapas Theater Kitchen," swanky dining room and lively bar, Tavern N' Town is considered to be one of Key West's top dining destinations. Inspired dishes, like this recipe for Cilantro-Seared Swordfish by Executive Chef Rodrigo Alvarez, make it one of our favorite places to indulge.

INGREDIENTS
(Yield 1 Serving)
6 Oz Fresh Swordfish Steak
Cilantro Oil
1/2 Cup cooked, Julienned Red Beets
1/2 Cup Kale
2 Tbl Pancetta
1 Tbl Smoked Onion Butter
3 Tbl Caramelized Shallot Puree
1 Cup Beurre Blanc Sauce
Salt & Pepper to Taste
Merken Spice To taste

PREPARATION
Season swordfish with salt and pepper. Rub with cilantro oil. Pre-heat oven to 350°. In a hot sauté pan, sear swordfish on just one side. Transfer to pan and finish in the oven for 4 min. In separate hot pan, add pancetta, kale, garlic and merken spice. Cook until kale is soft and then add red beet. Finish with smoked onion butter. In small pan, warn up beurre blanc sauce, add caramelized shallot puree.

TO SERVE
Spoon beurre blanc into dish. Add kale and red beet mixture and top with swordfish steak.

You can find Tavern N' Town Restaurant at the the Marriott Key West Beachside Resort, 3811 N. Roosevelt Blvd. 305-296-8100; tavernntown.com.

Jonesing For Terrific Pasta?
Mangia, Mangia Pasta Cafe, Key West

While it's not always easy to find delicious gluten-free pasta in most restaurants, Mangia Mangia hits it out of the park with their high-protein Quinoa pasta. Top the pasta with their tasty marinara (or any of their other beautiful sauces); it's hard to beat.

Lots of grilled specialties here, too, along with beef, seafood, organic chicken, vegetarian, and gluten/egg-free dishes.

A seductive and extensive wine list features vintages dating back to the 1950s and has received Wine Spectator's Award of Excellence.

You can find Mangia Mangia at 900 Southard Street in Old Town Key West. Open daily from 5:30 - 10 pm. Info and reservations: 305-294-2469; mangia-mangia.com.

Renowned for the impeccable fresh homemade pasta and made-from-scratch, herb-spiked sauces, this cozy Chicago-style trattoria is one of Key West's best values. It serves up simple, full flavors that are intoxicatingly good.

You can't go wrong with anything on the menu here. Our picks include the Spaghettini with green-lipped New Zealand Mussels in a garlicky marina sauce. The heavenly Seafood Scampi with Maine lobster, shrimp, and lump blue crab; and the full-flavored Fettuccine with pine nut and walnut pesto.

RIGATONI WITH JUMBO SHRIMP

Mangia Mangia Pasta Cafe, Key West

Here in Key West, Mangia Mangia is famous for their fresh homemade pasta and feel-good neighborhood vibe. One of our most favorite pasta dishes is the Rigatoni with Jumbo Shrimp. Here's how to make it right at home.

INGREDIENTS
(Yield 1 Serving)
5 Jumbo Shrimp
1 Oz Extra Virgin Oil Oil
1/2 Oz Fresh Garlic, chopped
8 Oz Fresh Rigatoni
1 Oz Prosciutto
4-5 Black Olives, chopped
1 Oz Shallots, chopped
1 Oz Fresh Chopped Tomato
1-2 Shakes of Red Pepper
1/2 Oz Romano Cheese

PREPARATION
Cook Rigatoni as directed. Sauté shrimp in olive oil with the prosciutto, garlic, black olives, shallots, tomato and red pepper for approximately 3 minutes or until shrimp are pink.

Remove and plate. Garnish with radicchio, arugula and Belgian endive. Top with a dusting of Romano cheese.

You can find Mangia Mangia Pasta Cafe, 900 Southard St, Key West
305-294-2469; mangia-mangia.com

FRIED CHICKEN
With Island Key Lime/Sour Orange & Garlic
By Key West's Evangeline Washington

Evangeline's note: My father was Joseph Russell who made his living as a cook for several well-known residents of Key West, including Ernest Hemingway, William Freeman and John Spottswood. Some of the recipes I prepare today were learned from my father, my Godmother and my mother, Lydia. I have changed them only slightly over the years. This is one of my favorites.

INGREDIENTS
2 Fresh 4 Lb Chickens
6 Large Key Limes, juiced
3 Sour Oranges, juiced
4 Large Cloves of Garlic, finely chopped
1 Tbl Red Cayenne Pepper
2 Eggs
1 Cup Whole Milk
Self-Rising Flour
Cooking Oil (Canola or Peanut Oil)

PREPARATION
Rinse chicken parts thoroughly and place in a large, non-reactive container (either a glass or plastic bowl). Combine juices of lime, orange, chopped garlic, black and red pepper and pour over the chicken. Cover tightly with plastic wrap and marinate in the refrigerator overnight. When ready to cook, remove chicken from refrigerator, allowing enough time for chicken to come to room temperature. Meanwhile, combine eggs and milk. Place flour and pepper to taste in a brown paper bag. Dip chicken parts in egg mixture until thoroughly coated. Place in brown paper bag, a few pieces at a time. Shake bag until chicken parts are completely coated with flour. Heat oil to 350 degrees. Slowly place chicken in hot oil, a few pieces at a time, and fry until cooked.

Be careful not to cook chicken too quickly. Place on paper towels to drain excess oil. Serve immediately with black beans and rice and your favorite green salad.

Evangeline Washington originally donated this recipe for a fundraiser cookbook benefiting Key West's Bahama Village Music Program.
To donate to this wonderful organization, please go to BVMPKW.org

ISLAND SHRIMP CAKES
Square Grouper Bar & Grill, Cudjoe Key

Considered to be one of the Keys' Top "Must Visit" restaurants, Square Grouper Bar & Grill has a reputation for innovative local seafood preparations, house-made desserts, eclectic boutique wines and unusual craft beer. Chef/owner Lynn Bell never ceases to amaze us with all of her fabulous specials. Here's the recipe:

INGREDIENTS
(Yield 24 Cakes)
4 Lb Cooked, Cleaned and Chopped Shrimp (16/20s)
1 Cup Chopped Red Onion
1 Cup Chopped Red Pepper
1 Cup Minced Banana Pepper
1/8 Cup Minced Jalepenos
Zest From Two Lemons
5 Eggs, Beaten
1-1/2 Cups Fresh Lemon Juice
1-1/2 Cups Mayonnaise
2 Tsp. Tabasco Sauce
3 Tbl. Old Bay Seasoning
Add Panko Crumbs to Bind (Approx. 2 Quarts)

PREPARATION
Combine all of the ingredients. Form into cakes. Seat, bake at 425° for 10 minutes. Serve with lemon wedge and Island Pepper Aioli (recipe follows).

ISLAND PEPPER AIOLI
2 Cups Mayonnaise
1/4 Cup Minced Banana Peppers
1/8 Cup Pickled Jalapenos Minced
1 Tbl. Key Lime Juice
1 Tbl. Minced Garlic

PREPARATION
Combine all the above and season with salt and pepper to taste.

You can find Square Grouper at MM 80.4, Bayside in Islamorada (786-901-5678) and at MM 22.5 on Cudjoe Key. 305-745-880; squaregrouperbarandgrill.com

TAKO-YAKINIKU
Kaiyo Grill & Sushi, Islamorada

Islamorada's award-winning Kaiyo Grill & Sushi is one of our all-time favorite restaurants. We especially love this recipe for wood-grilled local octopus with fennel shallot and Fuji apple sunomono salad garnished with a grilled Meyer lemon.

SUNOMONO SALAD
(Pickled Cucumber)
3 European cucumbers cut in half with seeds removed
1 Fennel Bulb, shaved
1 Fuji Apple, shaved
1 Shallot, shaved

PREPARATION
Mix all ingredients with rice vinegar, sugar and salt to taste. Let stand ten minutes. Strain and set aside.

Chef's Tip: Remaining liquid mixed with olive oil makes a great vinaigrette!

WOOD-FIRE GRILLED OCTOPUS
(Yield 4 Servings)
2 Lbs. Fresh Octopus
6 Cups White Wine
8 Cups Water
1 Shallot, chopped
2 Garlic Cloves, chopped
1 Orange, squeezed
1 Lemon, squeezed
1 Lime, squeezed

MARINADE
Olive Oil
Lemon Juice
Spanish Paprika

tasty!

PREPARATION
Thoroughly clean octopus by first removing the ink sack and head. Discard any outer residue using a dry towel or fine brush. Bring all other ingredients to to heavy simmer in a large pot and then quickly dip the octopus three to four times to temper before completely immersing. (This prevents the tentacles from toughening and also keeps the nice purple skin intact.) Simmer about 45 min or until the tentacles are curled inward towards the body. Remove and chill. Marinate in olive oil, lemon juice and Spanish paprika for approximately four hours. Remove the octopus from the marinade. Grill on high heat, frequently turning to get an even char on both sides. Remove from grill, season with salt and pepper and drizzle with olive oil. To serve, cut octopus into small edible cuts and arrange on serving platter with 2-3 oz of the sunomono salad and grilled lemon. Squeeze the lemon over the octopus and enjoy!!!

You can find Kaiyo Grill & Sushi at MM 81.7, Oceanside, Islamorada
305-664-5556; KaiyoGrill.com

Keys Eats

SWEET TREATS

KRISTI'S TROPICAL RUM CAKE

Olive Morada, Islamorada

Wow the crowd with this rich, spirited Tropical Rum Cake made with Olive Morada's Persian Lime Olive Oil & Coconut Balsamic. A hefty dose of rum gives it just enough kick! You can also pick up all kinds of other Extra Virgin Olive Oils and Vinegars at this cool little shop along with lots of other gourmet foods and unique gifts.

INGREDIENTS FOR CAKE
1 Yellow Cake Mix
1/2 Cup Water
4 Eggs
1/3 Cup Olive Morada Persian Lime Olive Oil
1/2 Cup Dark Rum (or substitute 4 Tbs of rum extract)
1/4 Cup Olive Morada Coconut Balsamic Vinegar
1 Package (3.4oz) Instant Vanilla Pudding

CAKE PREPARATION
Preheat oven to 350°. Mix all ingredients in a bowl. Pour into Bundt cake pan and bake for approximately 30 - 35 minutes.

INGREDIENTS FOR GLAZE
1 Stick of Butter
1 Cup of Sugar
1/4 Cup of Water
1/2 Cup of Rum

GLAZE PREPARATION
While cake is baking, prepare glaze on stove top. Bring butter, sugar and water to a boil. Add rum and bring to a second boil. When cake is finished baking, remove from oven and pour glaze over it while still in the Bundt pan. Once cooled, flip over onto plate and enjoy!

You can find Olive Morada at 82245 Overseas Hwy Islamorada
305-735-4375; olivemorada.com

EASY PEASY CREAMY MANGO PIE

Mango Fest, Key West

If you've never experienced eating a creamy mango pie, you are in for a real treat. Whip up this super easy recipe for a forkful of summer.

CRUST INGREDIENTS
1-1/2 Cups Graham Crackers, finely crushed (about 12 full sheets of graham crackers)
1/3 Cup Granulated Sugar
6 Tbl Melted Butter

FILLING INGREDIENTS
4 Egg Yolks
1 Can (14 oz) Sweetened Condensed Milk
3/4 Cup Fresh Mango Puree* (instructions follow)
2 Tbl Fresh Lime Juice

TOPPING INGREDIENTS
2 Cups Cold Heavy Cream
1/3 Cup Granulated Sugar
1 Cup Unsweetened Coconut Flakes, toasted**

PREPARATION
Heat oven to 350°F. In a large bowl, stir graham cracker crumbs, 1/3 cup sugar and butter until well combined. Firmly press mixture evenly into bottom and up sides of 9-inch pie plate. Bake 8-10 minutes until lightly browned. Cool completely on a cooling rack. Reduce oven temperature to 325°F.

In a separate large bowl using an electric hand mixer on high speed, beat egg yolks 3-4 minutes until thick, creamy and pale yellow. Add sweetened condensed milk; beat on medium-high speed another 2 minutes. Stir in mango puree and lime juice until well combined.

Pour and spread mango mixture evenly into bottom of fully cooled crust. Bake 25-30 minutes until center of mango mixture is just set. If crust is getting too brown, cover edges with foil. Transfer pie to cooling rack to cool completely, about 1 hour. Cover and refrigerate. Just before serving, make the whipped cream topping: In a large bowl using an electric hand mixer on high speed, beat heavy cream and 1/3 cup sugar until stiff peaks form. Spread whipped cream evenly over top of pie. Sprinkle with toasted coconut.

*Notes
*To make mango puree, blend peeled and chopped fresh or frozen mango until smooth. If frozen, let mango puree come to room temperature before using. **To toast coconut flakes: Heat oven to 350°F. Spread coconut flakes evenly on rimmed baking sheet. Toast in oven 3-5 minutes, stirring every 2 minutes, until lightly browned.

Looking for more tasty mango recipes? Find more at mangofestkeywest.com

Key Lime Pie Addict
David Sloan

David Sloan is one colorful dude who's hard to define. Author, baker, ghost hunter, and co-founder of Key West's Key Lime Festival, David always seems to have the Midas Touch, especially when it comes to Key lime pie.

His book, the "Key West Key Lime Pie Cookbook," features recipes for twenty crusts, fillings, sauces, and toppings — all of which can be mixed and matched to create more than 150,000 varieties of Key lime pie.

But David's connection with Key lime pie didn't start or end with his cookbook. He began as a young boy back in Texas where he honed his skills, making thousands of Key lime pies for a local hamburger joint and then escalated decades later when he heard about a Key Lime Festival in Key Largo that happened in the 1950s.

That's all it took. In July 2013, and with great fanfare, David and his cohorts launched their own Key West Key Lime Festival with all kinds of crazy events, including a "Miss Key Lime" pageant, a Key lime pie-eating contest and the creation of the world's most massive Key lime pie.

The festival takes place annually over the 4th of July Weekend is always a "Sloan-Worthy" event. Find out more at keylimefestival.com.

AUTHENTIC KEY LIME PIE

Pepe's Cafe, Key West

Pepe's Cafe makes the favorite Key lime pie of David Sloan, author of the Ultimate Key Lime Pie Cookbook. According to Sloan, rather than just using egg yolks like a classic Key lime pie, "They use some egg white with the condensed milk. It makes it a little fluffier, very nice."

INGREDIENTS FOR CRUST
1 1/4 Cups Graham Cracker Crumbs from 12 (2 1/4-inch by 4 3/4-inch) crackers
1/4 Cup Sugar
1 Tsp Ground Cinnamon
5 Tbl. Unsalted Butter, melted

FOR FILLING
1 14-oz Can Sweetened Condensed Milk
2 Large Egg Whites
4 Large Egg Yolks
1/2 Cup Fresh or Bottled Key Lime Juice

FOR TOPPING
1 Cup Chilled Heavy Cream
3 Tbl Confectioner's Sugar

PREPARATION FOR THE CRUST
Arrange rack in the middle of the oven and preheat to 350°F. Stir together graham cracker crumbs, sugar and cinnamon. Drizzle with the melted butter and stir well. Press mixture evenly onto bottom and up the sides of a 9-inch (4-cup) glass pie plate. Bake crust about 10 minutes until golden brown. Remove pie from oven and transfer plate to a wire rack to cool. Leave oven on.

PREPARATION FOR THE FILLING:
In the bowl of a stand mixer fitted with the whisk attachment, or in a large mixing bowl with a whisk or hand mixer, beat the egg whites until they hold stiff peaks. In a large mixing bowl, whisk together the egg yolks and sweetened condensed milk. Add the lime juice and whisk until combined. Gently fold in about 1/3 of the egg whites to lighten the mixture then add the remaining egg whites and fold until just evenly combined. Gently spread the mixture in the pre-baked crust and bake until just set in the center, about 20 minutes.

TO SERVE
Transfer to a wire rack to cool completely, then refrigerate at least 2 hours before serving. Beat heavy cream and sugar together in a mixer until stiff peaks form. Spread or pipe the whipped cream on top of the cooled pie. The pie can be stored, covered, in the refrigerator, up to 3 days.

Pepe's Cafe is located at 806 Caroline St, Key West, 305-294-7192
You can also find signature variations of this iconic dessert throughout the Keys.

BANANA BREAD
Lazy Lobster, Key Largo

For more than two decades, Chef/Owner Lupe Ledesma has been treating his ardent followers to his special homemade banana bread which includes the addition of coconut along with a drizzle of chocolate. It's not unusual for his restaurant to go through three batches of this house favorite on a busy day.

INGREDIENTS
(Yield 16 Loaves - 6 slices per loaf)
8 Large Bananas, peeled and mashed
8 Large Eggs, beaten
2 Cups Vegetable Oil, plus more for pan
4 Cups Sugar
5 Cups All-Purpose Flour
1 Tbl Baking Powder
1 Tbl Baking Soda
2 Tsp Salt
2 Tsp Cinnamon
2 Tsp Vanilla
½ Cup Coconut
½ Cup Chopped Walnuts
½ Cup Hershey's Chocolate Syrup

PREPARATION
Heat oven to 350° F. Grease 8-ounce miniature loaf pans, set aside. Using a large bowl, combine bananas, eggs and oil. Add the sugar, mixing until combined. Add the flour, baking powder, baking soda, salt and cinnamon, mixing just until combined. Add the vanilla, coconut and walnuts. Divide batter between prepared pans. Drizzle a line of chocolate syrup on the top of each pan. Run a knife through the syrup into the batter in a swirling motion. Bake until top of loaf bounces back when lightly touched in center, about 40-45 minutes. Cool on a wire rack for 10 minutes. Invert pans on wire rack and cool completely.

You can find the Lazy Lobster at 102770 Overseas Hwy (MM 102, Bayside) in Key Largo. 305-451-0656; lazylobsterinthekeys.com

PUFFINS PANCAKE MINI-MUFFINS
With Artisan Maple Syrup And Pecans
Firefly, Key West

New American food with a Southern twist is the hallmark of this relaxed, Bahama Village hang. The Chefs here throw caution to the wind creating some of the most modern, innovative dishes you'll find in Key West.

FOR THE MUFFINS
(Yield Six Servings)
1.5 Cup All Purpose Flour
2 Tbl Sugar
2 Tsp Baking Powder
1/2 Tsp Salt
2 Large Eggs
1.5 Cups Milk
3 Tbl Melted Butter

TO FINISH THE MUFFINS
2 Tbl Unsalted Butter
2 Tbl Sugar
1 Oz Bourbon

FOR THE PLATE
3 Bananas cut on bias
(about 10 slices per banana)
1/2 Cup Chopped Pecans
1/4 Cup Brown Sugar
Small Handful Mint for Garnish
Maple Syrup

MUFFIN PREPARATION
Set oven to 350°. Add all dry ingredients together in one bowl. Whisk together all wet ingredients in another. Slowly whisk the wet ingredients into the dry ingredients until the batter is smooth. Grease the cups of a small to medium muffin pan and fill the cups halfway with the mix. Bake 12-15 minutes or until the top is golden brown and a tooth pick comes out clean. Remove the muffins from the tin and set aside.

PECANS PREPARATION
Toss the pecans with brown sugar. Place on a sheet pan covered with parchment paper and bake at 350° until the pecans are fragrant.

ASSEMBLY
Heat the butter and sugar in a pan on low to medium heat until the butter is melted. Add the muffins to the pan. When they start to get slightly browned, add the bourbon. Carefully ignite the alcohol in the pan, allow to burn until it dissipates. Remove muffins and place them on a plate. Add the sliced bananas and top with the pecans. Add maple syrup and garnish with mint. *Enjoy!*

You can find firefly at 222 Petronia St in Key West
305-849-0104; fireflykeywest.com

Foodie Happenings
Florida Keys & Key West

There's never a dull moment down here in Paradise because there is always something going on. Here's a month-by-month calendar of major food-related events that have become longstanding traditions.

JANUARY

KEY WEST FOOD & WINE FESTIVAL
Key West: Celebrate the local culinary arts community and enjoy lots of lively events all over the island, including a Welcome Beach Party, Wine Dinners, Shrimp Boil, Wine & Food Seminars, Bad Ass Brunches, "Duval Uncorked," Neighborhood Wine Strolls, Grand Tasting, and much more. Info: 305-292-1622.

UNCORKED FOOD & WINE FESTIVAL
Key Largo/Islamorada: Culinary experts step up to the palate for ten glorious days of food, wine, and spirited events. You can enjoy wine tastings and dinners, cooking demos, food and wine pairing classes, art and wine shows, a Gospel Brunch, and the Florida Keys' famous "Chopped" Charity Event. Info: 305-522-1300; floridakeysuncorked.com.

BAYGRASS BLUEGRASS & CRAFT BEER FESTIVAL
Islamorada: This weekend-long festival kicks off, mid-January "downtown" Islamorada on Fri, with a celebration along the Morada Way Arts & Cultural District. On Sat, a fun Pickin' Party & BBQ starts at 5 pm in Founders Park. The main concert, which happens on Sun, from 11 am - 8 pm, features a terrific blend of excellent Bluegrass music as well as a Craft Beer Garden and arts & crafts vendors. Info: baygrassbluegrass.com.

FLORIDA SEAFOOD FESTIVAL
Key West: Lots going on for both adults and kids from feasting on fresh local seafood and shopping for marine-related crafts, to face-painting, kids' hands-on activities, raffles, and live music. Takes place on Sat from 11 am - 8

pm and on Sun from 11 am - 5 pm in Bay View Park at 1320 Truman Ave. Info: 305-619-0039; floridakeysseafoodfestival.com.

MASTER CHEFS CLASSIC
Key West: Local chefs go head to head as they compete for Best of the Best in Appetizer, Entree, and Dessert categories as they provide a fantastic array of incredible food for those who are lucky enough to snag tickets. This event always sells out early and is a fundraiser for the MARC House. The event takes place from 4 - 7 pm at Margaritaville Key West Resort & Marina, 245 Front St. Info: 305-294-9526; masterchefsclassic.com.

FEBRUARY

FOOD TRUCK FESTIVAL
Key West: The Key West Art & Historical Society plays host to this family-friendly musical feast that showcases the grooving tunes of local and international acts as well as top-notch food trucks. Takes place from noon - 7 pm at Fort East Martello parade grounds.

VALENTINE'S DAY CHAMPAGNE & APHRODISIACS SUNSET SAIL
Key West: Celebrate Valentine's Day aboard the romantic Schooner America 2.0. with an oh-so-special Champagne and Aphrodisiacs Pairing

Sunset Sail. You and your true love can sail along Key West's beautiful turquoise green waters, sipping delicious champagnes and sparkling wines from around the world paired with a titillating selection of gourmet hors d'oeuvres. Ooh-La-La! Find it on the docks behind Schooner Wharf Bar in Key West's Historic Seaport. Info and reservations: 305-293-7245; sail-keywest.com.

WESLEY HOUSE VALENTINE'S DAY GALA

Key West: This heartfelt block party doubles as a fundraiser for Wesley House Family Services and includes top entertainers, the island's largest silent auction, open bar, dancing, and a lavish buffet dinner. Takes place from 6:30-9:30 pm at Key West's historic Curry Inn, 511 Caroline St., Key West. Reservations and info: 305-809-5000. keystix.com.

MARCH

ORIGINAL MARATHON SEAFOOD FESTIVAL

Marathon: The signature culinary and family event celebrates the Keys' bounty with all kinds of gourmet delicacies from the waters of the Florida Keys. Live music, an open-air art show, and lots of vendor booths make for a delectable weekend. Open Sat from 10 am – 9 pm and on Sun from 11 am – 5 pm. Takes place at Marathon Community Park, MM 49, Oceanside. Info: 305-743-5417; floridakeysmarathon.com.

ISLAMORADA SEAFOOD FEST & ART SHOW

Islamorada: This lively, hometown festival is a local favorite and always draws fun crowds who take to the street for a day of yummy fresh seafood, culinary delights, fine art, crafts, and jammin' entertainment. Takes place from 11 am - 5 pm in the Morada Way Arts & Cultural District at MM 81 on Old Hwy., Islamorada. Info: 305-664-8120.

KEY COLONY BEACH DAY

Key Colony Beach: This old fashioned, annual event draws a local island crowd who gather for a lazy day of good food, drinks, and music. Start with the Shriners' Pancake Breakfast at 8 am, stroll the art and crafts booths, try your luck at the world-famous barracuda races, or bet on your favorite plastic ducky in a "swim" against all the odds across the 7th Street Canal. Free admission and parking. It takes place from 8 am - 4 pm at City Hall Park, Key Colony Beach. Info: KCBCA.org

APRIL

FLORIDA KEYS ISLAND FEST

Islamorada: Two full days of music, food, and fun including one of the largest crafts shows in the Keys, live entertainment, sandcastle-building, kids' activities, and the annual "Taste Of Islamorada" — a local chefs' competition which happens on Sunday. Free admission. Takes place from 10 am - 5 pm at Founder's Park, MM 87, Bayside, Islamorada. Info: 305-664-4503; islamoradachamber.com.

Foodie Happenings

TASTE OF KEY WEST
Key West: Over 50 top area restaurants and 100+ vineyards present mouthwatering samples of their cuisine to benefit AIDS Help, Inc. Food and wine tickets cost $1 with "tastes" ranging from $3 - $8. The culinary celebration takes place from 6 - 9 pm at the Truman Waterfront Pier (end of Southard St.) overlooking Key West Harbor. Free admission. Info: 305-296-6196.

MAY

KEY WEST WHISKEY FEST
Key West: Enjoy this new celebration dedicated to top class whiskeys. Highlights include a big kick-Off Party, a wide range of tastings, Whiskey Walks, Workshops, Brunches and much more. Info: 305-509-9775; keywestwhiskeyfest.com.

JUNE

MANGO FEST KEY WEST
Key West: It's four days of "Mango Madness" during this tasty annual event that includes mango tasting, mango trees, and mango daiquiris. The culinary competitions between local chefs and residents alike showcases the colorful abilities of what the mango, also known as the king of fruit, has to offer. The Vendor Village gives art collectors and foodies the experience of a festival atmosphere. Music is provided along with live radio broadcasts. It takes place from 10 am to 3 pm at Bayview Park, 1400 Truman Ave. Info: 305-809-3874; mangofestkeywest.com.

JULY

KEY LIME FESTIVAL
Key West: A crazy "Mile High" pie-eating contest, Key Lime Pie Hop, Key Lime Rum Sampling, Cooking Lessons, and other tasty temptations are all on the menu for this wacky, 4th of July weekend event that kicks off with a Key Lime Sip & Stroll. Complete event schedule at keylimefestival.com.

HOSPICE & VNA JULY 4 PICNIC
Key West: This annual family-friendly, beachside picnic is also a fundraiser for Monroe County's Hospice with an endless supply of hot dogs and hamburgers, top entertainment, silent auction, children's activities, and a giant fireworks display off the White Street Pier by Higgs Beach. VIP seating on the beach available. Takes place on the lawn and beach of the historic Casa Marina Resort, 1500 Reynolds St. Info: 305-294-8812.

MINI-LOBSTER SEASON
Every Mini Lobster season, the coastal areas of Florida are flooded with lobster hunters trying to get their share of this year's bounty. There are two Florida Lobster Seasons, the two-day mini-season, and the eight-month regular lobster season. The mini lobster season is always the last consecutive Wednesday and Thursday in July.

AUGUST

KEY WEST LOBSTERFEST
Key West: It's a weekend of "Lobstermania" when approximately 10,000 pounds of succulent, locally caught lobster is grilled, sautéed, stuffed and deliciously prepared to celebrate the bounty of the Keys lobster season. Lots of activities all weekend long. Info: 305-294-2000; keywestlobsterfest.com.

KEY WEST BREWFEST
Key West: More than 150 beers and craft brews are on tap at this "tasty" annual event that includes beer dinners, beer brunches, Happy Hour parties, pool parties, late-night parties, seminars, and the Signature Tasting Festival Event on Saturday. Info: 800-354-4455; keywestbrewfest.com.

NOVEMBER

MARRVELOUS PET RESCUES "SPAY-GHETTI & NO BALLS HOLIDAY GALA"

Key Largo: This fun annual dinner, auction and mega dance party benefits MarrVelous Pet Rescues, dedicated to uniting pets with loving homes and families. Takes place at 6:30 pm on the waterfront at the beautiful Snook's Bayside Restaurant & Grand Tiki, MM 99.9 Bayside, Key Largo. Tickets are EXTREMELY limited and not sold at the door. Info and tickets: 305-453-1315; spayghetti.com.

TASTE OF THE ISLANDS

Marathon: This award-winning event draws several thousand attendees and features local restaurants, live entertainment, vendors, and artists, a tribute to veterans, fashion show, kids' activities, plus live and Chinese auctions. Takes place from 11 am - 5 pm at Marathon Community Park, MM 49, oceanside, Marathon. Info: 305-923-9976.

KEY LARGO CHAMBER OF COMMERCE COOK-OFF

Key Largo: This legendary culinary competition challenges both professional and amateur cooks and chefs, as well as young aspiring chefs to create their very best soups and chowders, appetizers, main dishes, sides, and salads, as well as desserts. Takes place from 6 - 8:30 pm at the Holiday Inn, MM100, Oceanside in Key Largo. Tickets: Key Largo Chamber of Commerce. Info: 305-451-4747; keylargochamber.org.

DECEMBER

"I LOVE STOCK ISLAND" FESTIVAL

Key West: Celebrate Stock Island's culture and heritage with three great days of the very best Stock Island has to offer, including music, foodie events, wine, beer & rum pairings, history & art studio tours, water sports, and fresh straight-off-the-boat seafood! Takes place on Stock Island. Info: 573-680-5468; ilovestockisland.org.

FLORIDA KEYS HOLIDAY FESTIVAL

Islamorada: A 35' holiday tree blows magical snow at this festive extravaganza, which includes a parade, caroling, holiday gift bazaar, delicious food, Vino Village, live music, and a silent  auction of masterpiece ornaments created by local artists. Takes place from 4 - 10 pm at Founders Park, MM 87, Bayside. Info: 305-664-4503; islamoradachamber.com.

NOCHE BUENA - CHRISTMAS EVE FEAST

Key West: Why go to a restaurant on Christmas Eve when you can enjoy a real Key West family dinner? "Noche Buena" is a long-celebrated tradition in Latin communities and is proudly celebrated in Key West by local families. Local resident Wayne Garcia and his family will be serving up a traditional menu of Roast Pork, Black Beans and Rice, Plantains, and postre. Takes place from 6 - 10 pm in Lily's Garden at the Oldest House Museum, 322 Duval St. Info: 305-294-9501; oirf.org.

GINGERBREAD HOUSE MAKING PARTY

Key West: Get your gingerbread on during this free, hands-on event that takes cookie making to a whole new level. Takes place from 11 am - 3 pm in Lily's Garden at the Oldest House Museum, 322 Duval St. Info: 305-294-9501; oirf.org.

UNCORKED!

Key Largo & Islamorada Food & Wine Festival

Uncorked - the Key Largo & Islamorada Food & Wine Festival which takes place in mid-January, rolls out the red carpet with ten glorious days of more than 37 wine tasting events, cooking demos, progressive wine dinners, live music, food and wine pairing classes, art & wine shows and more.

Other event highlights include the Keys version of the popular television cooking show "Chopped" to benefit local charities as well as multiple themed "How-To" cooking events.

On "Festival Saturday," Islamorada's beautiful Postcard Inn & Marina, MM 84, sets a spectacular oceanfront stage for the festival's "Grand Tasting." A fabulous afternoon event where you can sample signature dishes by local chefs, sip on world-class wines, and pop your cork to some terrific live music.

For event info and tickets, call 305-522-1300 or go to FloridaKeysUncorked.com.

Wine Down in Key West

Key West Food & Wine Festival

If you love food and wine as much as we do, book your trip to Key West right now and get down to Key West for the annual Food & Wine Festival, which happens every year during the last week in January.

With gourmet galas and tastings, tours and seminars, parties and lots of tasty "only in Key West experiences," this foodie extravaganza will simply blow you away.

One of the Festival's most significant events (and our personal favorite) is the highly anticipated Grand Tasting. The Grand Tasting, which takes place at a different location each year, includes delicious food, free-flowing vintage wines, and a commemorative wine glass etched with the Festival's distinct logo.

Another all-time favorite is "Uncorked," an adventurous afternoon wine stroll from 2 - 5 pm on Festival Sunday that spans the length of Key West's renowned Duval Street.

Prepare yourself for this one because it's an over-the-top, mile-long "sipping and shopping" spree that will put you through your paces.

Other stand-out happenings include a Sunset Kick-Off Party, an Original Stock Island Shrimp Boil, food and wine seminars, wine pairings, party, and a whole lot more. Sound good? Then hit up keywestfoodandwinefestival.com and find out all the deets.

Cheers!

Feast Your Eyes On This
Original Marathon Seafood Festival

If it's March, it must be time for the the Original Marathon Seafood Festival!

For over four decades, this affordable foodie-fair, which takes place every winter, celebrates the bounty of local fishermen with gourmet delicacies from the waters of the Florida Keys.

The 15,000 pounds (yes 15 THOUSAND pounds!) of fresh, succulent seafood served here is caught, cleaned, and cooked by local commercial fishermen who also prepare bushels of oysters and bags of clams from the west coast of Florida.

Scores of community volunteers serve up generous plates during this "Fisherman-to-Fork" feast as local chefs showcase their talents using their Keys-based recipes.

Of course, Florida spiny lobster, with beans, bread, butter, and coleslaw, is a festival staple. Still, you can also indulge in other favorite indigenous offerings like mahi-mahi, Key West pink shrimp, stone crab claws, smoked fish dip, and much more.

Conch lovers can also have it every which way: as ceviche, chowder, golden-fried fritters, or as bun-hugging "konkwurst" sausage.

There are lots of landlubber offerings, too, including hamburgers, hot dogs, sausages with sides of baked beans, coleslaw, hush puppies and French fries.

Popular Keys entertainers are always on hand, as well, along with more than 200 vendor booths, a Keys Artist Village, boat show, and art exhibition.

Eat your heart out on Festival Saturday from 10 am to 9 pm and on Festival Sunday from 11 am to 5 pm at Marathon Community Park, MM 49, Bayside, Marathon. Info at 800-262-7284; marathonseafoodfestival.com.

Spring Grooves In Islamorada
Florida Keys Island Fest

Here in the Keys, Springtime means taking in lots of fun outdoor events, concerts, and festivals. One of our particular favorites is the annual Florida Keys Island Fest, which takes place at Islamorada's Founders Park (MM 87) in late March or early April.

If you've never been to this beautiful bayside respite, this is a perfect time to check it out.

During this fun two day celebration, the park and beach areas transform into an outdoor musical, artistic and green-market emporium with over 100 exceptional local and national artists, food vendors, and terrific live entertainment.

What we like about this Festival is that the artwork and handicrafts are not only top quality but are also really affordable, which makes it a great place to pick up a unique Keys keepsake.

Besides strolling the art show and grooving to live music, you can take in an old-fashioned All-American Road Vintage Cruisers Car Show, showcasing some very cool cars, trucks, motorcycles and rat rods. Kids can also have their beachside fun painting, building sand sculptures, and competing in hula-hoop contests beneath kite-filled skies.

One of the weekend's unique highlights is Saturday's wacky "What Floats Your Boat" race, where a fleet of homemade "boats" sets sail from the beach and struggles to stay above water. This event is always a real hoot and is later followed by a bayside concert from 5-7 pm at the park's waterfront amphitheater.

Needless to say, Festival Saturday is always lots of fun, but truth be told, our favorite day is Sunday during the annual "Taste Of Islamorada." This friendly culinary competition between local restaurants is your chance to sample lots of scrummy appetizers, entrees, and desserts. If you're a dedicated foodie like we are, be sure to buy plenty of "tasting" tickets because you'll have a lot of delectable bites to choose from.

Festival events take place rain or shine on Saturday from 10 am to 7:30 pm and on Sunday from 10 am to 5 pm.

Admission is free, and there's on-site parking available for a small $5 donation. BTW:

Organizers suggest that you bring lawn chairs and blankets so that you can fully enjoy the beach and concert.

For more info, call 305-664-4503 or hit up islamoradachamber.com.

Celebrating Sweet Summer

Mango Fest Key West

Summer comes but once a year and with it, the bounty of the island's burgeoning mango trees. Each June, we celebrate this annual harvest with Mango Fest Key West. This fun, fruitful event benefits the Key West Police Athletic Activities League and is one of the Keys' most significant fund-raisers for kids.

The annual festival features all things mango and takes place in late June when the island's mango trees are bursting with clusters of the juicy fruit.

There is always a fantastic array of activities going on, including culinary competitions and demonstrations, mango tastings, mango recipes with everything from tropical drinks to tacos and guacamole, poetry and prose contest, music, and more.

And get this: even if you're not going to be in Key West for the live event, you can still enjoy this far-out festival, virtually.

That's right, VIRTUALLY.

Festival organizer, Mark Certonio of Dolce Events, employs 360-degree photography of Key West's Truman Waterfront to create a Virtual "Mango Mania" Vendor Village that appears just as it would if you were there.

Imagine being able to "stroll" along the Key West waterfront where you can visit vendors and art galleries, order great food and even shop our local boutiques — all from the comfort of your home.

Want to learn how to create intriguing mango dishes, make the best Mango Mojito north of Havana, or shake things up with a Mango Margarita? Just tune in to one of the many culinary and cocktail videos that start each day at noon during the festival. There's a whole week's worth of fun happenings that are just a click away. Sound delicious? Get more deets at mangokeywest.com.

Really, it's the next best thing to being there!

AMERICA'S FAVORITE CITRUS CELEBRATION!

Key West's Key Lime Festival

Birthplace of the original Key Lime Pie, Key West is also home to the Annual Key Lime Festival which generally runs every 4th of July weekend.

Citrus, eccentrics, people, and pie take center stage during this wacky four-day celebration that is packed with culinary events for every taste.

Favorite happenings like the Key Lime Cocktail Sip & Stroll and Key Lime Pie Hop are a staple on the roster, along with the Key Lime Pie Drop and Key Lime Scavenger Hunt.

Other favorites include, The Key Limes & Coffee Guest Speaker Series features presentations on key lime cultivation and history from local experts.

The Key Lime University where you can learn to make key lime pies and cocktails.

A Key Lime Cookbook Signing & Champagne Reception by festival co-founder, chef, columnist and author, David Sloan who makes guest appearances throughout the festival.

Of course, the festival's undisputed highlight is the Mile-High Key Lime Pie Eating Contest.

Brave contestants must attempt to devour an entire pie, topped with mounds of whipped cream, without using their hands — while trying to outpace their rivals and beat the pie-eating record of 62 seconds. Admission is free, but if you're up to the task, the entry fee is just $20, which includes a lifetime of notoriety, a Key Lime Pie, and a chance to be a champion.

To register and see a full schedule of events, go to keylimefestival.com

After all, what's more American than Key Lime Pie?

NO CLAWS REQUIRED!

Key West Lobsterfest

For over two decades, Key West has celebrated the opening of Lobster Season (August 6 - March 31) by throwing the biggest party of the summer.

It always happens the first weekend after Lobster Season opens with a roster of events that you can sink your teeth into.

Famous for its sweet and tender meat, the Keys' spiny, clawless lobster is often served steamed with drawn butter, paired with a seasoned stuffing or in innovative dishes conceived by local chefs.

This weekend festival kicks off at 5 pm on Thursday when lobster aficionados gather for a traditional lobster boil at a designated location. Chow down on fresh lobster, jumbo shrimp, andouille sausage, corn on the cob, and more, backdropped by a gorgeous Key West sunset, live entertainment and drink specials.

The celebration continues on Friday with more parties and a lively Duval Pub Crawl that starts immediately after sunset and continues until midnight.

Things really crank up on Saturday with a Street Fair & Outdoor Concert, which takes place on the 100 - 500 blocks of Duval Street from noon to 11 pm.

Tons of artisans set up tents to sell their wares as over a dozen bars and restaurants dish up over 10,000 lbs of delicious, locally caught Lobster — from scrummy appetizers to full-blown dinners.

A free Saturday outdoor concert from 1-10:30 pm puts local performers on stage at the intersection of Duval and Greene streets.

Lobstermania weekend wraps up on Sunday with a decadent Lobster Brunch Buffet from 10 am — 2 pm at another designated location in Key West. Sound like fun?

Get this year's deets at keywestlobsterfest.com.

Keys Eats

UPPER KEYS

A MOVEABLE FEAST
Florida Keys Brewing
MM 81.5 Old Hwy
Islamorada, Fl 33036
305-304-0340;
flkeysfoodtruck.com
Chef-Inspired Food Truck
This "Feast Beast" on wheels serves up food truck fare with an inspired culinary spin. The revolving menu features signature specialties like global tacos, gourmet dogs, sausages, grilled cheese sandwiches, sliders, stuffed pretzel bites, and grilled pierogis. If you're having a get-together, the "Feast Beast" will even bring the party to you.

ATLANTIC EDGE RESTAURANT
At Cheeca Lodge
81801 Overseas Hwy (MM 82, Oceanside)
Islamorada, FL 33036
305-664-4651; cheeca.com
Open Daily 7 am — 10 pm
Gourmet Food & Island Romance
With stunning views of the Atlantic and both indoor and outdoor seating, this gracious landmark is renowned for its artfully prepared fresh local seafood, prime steaks, locally grown organic produce, a tantalizing array of house-made desserts and over 200 hand-picked select wines. Cited as one of "Florida's 500 Best Places to Dine" and honored with Wine Spectator's Award Of Excellence.

BAD BOY BURRITO
81868 Overseas Hwy
Islamorada, Fl 33036
305-509-7782; badboyburritoislamorada.com
M - Sa 10 am – 4 pm
Gourmet - Style Burritos
Recently featured on the Food Network, this local favorite is your "go-to" spot for the most authentic Mexican food in the Keys. Hot, salty, sweet Kobe Beef Burritos, Surf N' Turf Tacos, and melt-in-your-mouth carnitas are all made with fresh local ingredients.

Highly Recommended

BUZZARDS ROOST
Garden Cove Marina
21 Garden Cove Dr
(Just Off the Overseas Hwy at Card Sound Rd)
Key Largo, FL 33037
305-453-3746; buzzardsroostkeylargo.com
Open M-Su 11 am - 9 pm
Terrific Waterfront Hideaway
Named for Key Largo's high ground, called "Wachula," which means "buzzard's roost" in the native Seminole language, this intimate Keys hideaway overlooking Garden Cove Marina has some of the best food around. The fresh sautéed Lobster Reuben and the Corny Blue Crab Cakes are indeed Blue Ribbon worthy, and the house-made smoked fish dip, a unique blend of cold-smoked Mahi with cream cheese and spices, is a local favorite. Honestly, you just can't go wrong with any of the fresh seafood selections, and the certified Black Angus steaks are terrific. FYI: The Champagne Sunday Brunch here is also outstanding.

CIAO HOUND ITALIAN KITCHEN & BAR
84001 Overseas Hwy (MM 84 Oceanside)
Islamorada, Fl 33036
305-664-5300; ciaohound84.com
Su - Th 5 - 10pm; F & Sa 5 - 11pm
Relaxed Italian Dining
Islamorada's Italian kitchen pairs authentic Tuscan flavors with fresh Keys-sourced ingredients and Rat Pack-era tunes. The big menu includes lots of appetizers, salads, brick oven flatbreads, and sandwiches, along with an excellent selection of pasta, seafood, and house specialties. The oven-baked herb and parmesan-crusted Mahi-Mahi with crispy pancetta, rapini, and Marsala jus are especially delicious. Other favorites: pan sautéed Chicken Francese in lemon-white wine caper sauce; and the Ravioli Lobster: butter-tossed tomatoes, asparagus, and lobster chunks in brandy-paprika cream sauce. You'll also find a full bar that serves top-notch wines by the glass and bottle, local and imported beers, and nearly a dozen Italian-inspired cocktails. Added bonus: A Fido-friendly patio.

CAPT. CRAIG'S RESTAURANT
90154 Overseas Hwy
Tavernier, Fl 33070
305-852-9424; captcraigs.com
Daily 11 am — 10 pm
Good Food. Good Prices. Always Fresh.
Renowned for its "World Famous" Fresh Fish Sandwich, this casual roadside dig has been getting "two thumbs up" since it opened its doors in 1981. Favorites include Stone Crab Chowder, Shrimp Scampi, Key Lime Seafood, and Fried Seafood Baskets.

Keys Eats

CHEF MICHAEL'S ⊕
81671 Overseas Hwy (Old Highway)
Islamorada, Fl 33036
M - Sa 5 – 10 pm
305-664-0640; foodtotalkabout.com
Food to Really Talk About
New York City and Caribbean-trained owner/chef Michael Ledwith specializes in locally speared hogfish but also serves up fresh yellowtail, cobia, lionfish, and other locally sourced seafood — all to rave reviews. Try the tempura Maine lobster tail with buttery ginger and garlic dipping sauce. And don't overlook Michael's gourmet meat dishes, including Braised Lamb Shank, Peppered NY Strip Steak, and Crispy Roast Long Island Duck.

DIGIORGIO'S CAFE LARGO
99530 Overseas Hwy (MM 99.5 Bayside)
Key Largo, Fl 33037
305-451-4885; keylargo-cafelargo.com
Nightly 4:30 – 11 pm
"The "Little Italy" of the Upper Keys"
Chef/Owner Robert DiGiorgio's select menu of centuries-old family Italian specialties, pizzas, Certified Angus steaks and fresh, locally caught seafood dishes along with an extensive international wine list, has drawn local chefs and appreciative palates to his tables for over twenty years. Full bar with a cutting-edge, exotic liquor selection.

FISH HOUSE & SEAFOOD MARKET ⊕
102401 Overseas Hwy
(MM 102.4, Oceanside)
Key Largo, FL 33037
305-451-4665; fishhouse.com
Daily 11:30 am – 10 pm
Featured On The Food Network

Heralded by Fodor's, Zagat, Southern Living, and Travel & Leisure, this local landmark is famous for its "Conch-style" cooking and casual, "Old Keys" vibe. Fresh fish is the trademark here, brought in the back door daily by local fishermen, and filleted on-premises. FYI: The Baked Stuffed Catch with homemade blue crab stuffing is excellent, and the Key Lime Pie is as good as it gets!

GREEN TURTLE INN ⊕
81219 Overseas Hwy (MM 81.2, Oceanside)
Islamorada, FL 33036
305-664-2006; greenturtlekeys.com
Tu - Su 7 am -10 pm
Islamorada's Iconic Restaurant & Bar
This Islamorada icon is one of the Keys' most popular places to hang out. Locals flock here for the fabulous breakfast (served until 3 pm) as well as the inventive lunch and dinner fare, which includes fresh seafood, chops, steaks, and more. Signature dishes include Fresh Catch à la Roxie (fresh local fish, seared and topped with jumbo lump crab, tomato and sweet onion beurre blanc), and Fresh Catch à la Sid (fresh local fish, seared and covered in a Maine lobster, orange and vanilla butter sauce). The Black Angus Steak is also especially good. And if you like meatloaf, you must, must try the signature "Bacon-Wrapped Love" — mushroom-stuffed meatloaf wrapped in Applewood-smoked bacon with a tangy tomato glaze that was featured on the Food Network.

ISLAND GRILL
85501 Overseas Hwy (MM 85.5 Oceanside)
Islamorada, FL 33036
305-664-8400; keysislandgrill.com
Daily 7 am — 10 pm; Sa & Su 'till 11 pm
Home Of The Original Tuna Nachos
You can't beat this cool waterfront restaurant & beach bar for great island-style food and a fun Chiki-tiki atmosphere. The big, diverse menu includes stand-outs like the award-winning Tuna Nachos, Guava Ribs, Lobster Roll, Wasabi-Encrusted Catch & Seafood Pasta. Weddings and private events are a specialty here, and you can feast on everything from a Caribbean-style Pig Roast to a Parisian Seafood Buffet.

KAIYO GRILL & SUSHI ⊕
81701 Old US 1 Highway
Islamorada, FL 33036
305-664-5556; kaiyogrill.com
M - Sa 5 – 10 pm
Hip Dining Jewel
The land meets the sea at this popular Keys' landmark heralded for its fresh sushi, inventive wood-fire grilled specialties & connoisseur's wine list. The menu here is a notable collaboration by Kaiyo's celebrated chefs who have a special knack for creating rich, deeply flavored dishes with an Asian-Island twist. Kaiyo is one indulgent respite you don't want to miss.

KEY LARGO FISHERIES ⊕
1313 Ocean Bay Dr.
Key Largo, FL 33037
305-451-3782; keylargofisheries.com
Cafe: M-Sa 10 am – 8 pm
Market: 7 am -5:30 pm; F & Sa 'till 7 pm
Best Lobster BLT
Key Largo Fisheries is regarded as one of the Key's top wholesale seafood companies. This family-run Fishery also houses a renowned Retail Seafood Market, selling fresh seafood right off the docks, and a delightful outdoor "Backyard Café," where you can get terrific house-made specialties. Try their Conch Salad, Caesar Seafood Wraps, and

Fish Baskets. But, it's the chart-topping Lobster BLT & Lobster BLT Soup that will totally flip your flops!

LAZY DAYS
79867 Overseas Hwy (MM 79.9, Oceanside)
Islamorada, FL 33036
305-664-5256; lazydaysrestaurant.com
M - Su 11 am - 9:30 pm;
F & Sa 'till 10 pm
Award-Winning Favorite
Here's the perfect place to take in a beautiful oceanfront seascape and casually dine on award-winning Keys-style dishes, whether it's on the beach, on the patio, or inside the lively air-conditioned dining room. Interesting preparations of locally caught seafood, hand-cut steaks, and house specialties draw big local crowds and consistently win rave reviews. Top Pick: Grouper Lorenzo, served with crab cake and Key lime butter with house-made banana bread. FYI: The fish sandwich is also an absolute "Must!" Fish market and gift shop, too.

LAZY LOBSTER
79867 Overseas Hwy (MM 102, Bayside)
Key Largo, FL 33037
305-451-0565; lazylobsterinthekeys.com
Su - Th 11am - 9:30pm; F & Sa 11am - 10pm
A Wonderful Little Gem
Award-winning Chefs, Lupe Ledesma and David Ornelas, have brought their magical touch to this casual family-friendly eatery in Key Largo. And true to form, Chef Lupe and his team have another winner on their hands. The deep-fried lobster sandwich with jalapeño bread crust is just amazing. Other favorites: Wasabi-encrusted tuna, Shrimp Diablo, and Conch Ceviche - all are out of this world. Lupe's signature banana bread is also a staple here — yum!

LOR-E-LEI RESTAURANT
& CABANA BAR
81924 Overseas Hwy, Bayside
Islamorada, FL 33036
305-664-2692; loreleifloridakeys.com
M-Su 8 am – 11 pm
Best Keys Sunset Celebration
Home to the world-famous Lor-e-lei Back Country Fishing Guides, this casual family-friendly waterfront restaurant, and Cabana Bar has one of the best sunset views in the Keys. Lor-e-lei serves breakfast, lunch, and dinner seven days a week with nightly specials, fresh local seafood, and a variety of other delicious dishes. Live entertainment by local bands. Happy Hour specials from 4 - 6 pm.

MANGROVE MIKE'S CAFE
82200 Overseas Hwy
Islamorada, FL 33036
305-664-8022; mangrovemikes.com
Open M - Su 6 am – 2 pm
"Islamorada's "Best Breakfast Place"
"Mangrove Mike" Forster is a regular guy with a penchant for all things Keys. He's been flippin' flapjacks and serving up hearty homemade breakfasts and lunch since 1998 and his small family cafe is an everyday stop for locals who appreciate comfort cookin' at its best. Be sure to get there early. With enormous portions for under ten bucks, this locals' joint fills up fast! Full-service catering, too!

M.E.A.T EATERY & TAPROOM
88005 Overseas Hwy (MM 88, Oceanside)
Islamorada, FL 33036
305-664-0000; meateatery.com
Su - Th 11 am – 9 pm; F & Sa 11 am – 10 pm
Gourmet Fast-Casual Food
Award-winning Chef George Patti, and Uber Sommelier Tom Smith, have culled their talents once again to create this super cool "Eatery & Tap Room" where the house-ground and smoked sausages, non-traditional burgers and hot dogs take center stage. Boutique wines, unique craft beers, craft sodas, and adult "milkshakes" round out one of the edgiest casual menus in the Keys. Dine-in or take out.

MILE MARKER 88
8800 Overseas Hwy, Bayside
Islamorada, Fl 33036
305-852-9315; marker88.info
Daily 11 am — 10 pm; Su 10 am – 10 pm
Islamorada Landmark Restaurant
Overlooking the Florida Bay, this popular Islamorada landmark boasts spectacular sunset views and is known for its fresh, locally caught seafood. An array of Sushi Rolls top the list of yummy appetizers, which also includes all kinds of oyster preparations, coconut prawns, caviar, escargot, and conch fritters. Grouper, Snapper, and Mahi-Mahi can be prepared in nearly a dozen different ways. There's a good choice of landlubber entrees, as well. Be sure to save room for the critically-acclaimed Key Lime Pie and Baked Alaska.

Keys Eats

MORADA BAY BEACH CAFÉ & BAR
81600 Overseas Hwy
Islamorada, Fl 33036
305-664-0604; moradabay.com
Daily 11:30 am – 11 pm
Innovative, Eclectic American/Caribbean Fare

Super fresh, local seafood and produce are the stars of the show at this casually chic beach-front cafe, which sits directly on a glorious palm-studded beach. For a relaxing, kick-back meal in a picture-perfect setting, you found your place in the sun.

MRS. MAC'S KITCHEN
99336 Overseas Hwy, Bayside
Key Largo, Fl 33037
305-451-3722; mrsmacskitchen.com
M - Sa 7 am - 9:30 pm
Terrific Key Lime Pie

Mrs. Mac's has been serving up comfort food in the Keys since 1976. Antique license plates adorn the walls as well as the hanging lamps, which adds a fun touch to the eclectic tropical decor. The hearty house-made soups, salads, and seafood dishes keep the locals coming back, but it's always the Key lime pie that people rave about. They also have a second location at 99020 Overseas Hwy (on the median).

NIKAI
Cheeca Lodge
81801 Overseas Hwy (MM 82, Oceanside)
Islamorada, FL 33036
305-664-4651; cheeca.com
Nightly 6 – 10 pm
Intimate Sushi Restaurant

This ultra-cool Sushi Bar serves exceptional fresh sushi and Asian-inspired fare along with a unique selection of over 35 hot and cold Sakes, boutique wines, and tropical cocktails. Must Haves: The "Big Kahuna Roll" – tuna and avocado topped with lobster salad, macadamia nuts, and pineapple-ginger glaze; the "Dagwood Roll" – tempura shrimp and avocado topped with blue crab, tuna, sweet soy, and sesame seeds.

PIERRE'S LOUNGE & RESTAURANT
81600 Overseas Hwy
Islamorada, Fl 33036
305-664-3225; moradabay.com/pierres
Thu – Sun 6 – 10 pm; Fri & Sat 6 – 11 pm
French-Inspired Island Elegance

Nestled on the second floor of a magnificent plantation-style house, this "Islamorada Stunner" is renowned for its world-influenced French fusion cuisine. Everything on the menu is beautifully prepared and served in a romantic candlelit, 19th century "Indian Arcade," which is walled with extraordinary artifacts from Morocco and Africa. You can also enjoy a bite downstairs in the Green Flash Lounge or outside on the beautiful wrap-around veranda overlooking the beach and bay.

REEL BURGER
Amara Cay Resort
80001 Overseas Hwy
Islamorada, Fl 33036
305-664-0073
amaracayresort.com
Daily 11:30 am – 10 pm; Open
Daily 11:30 am — 10 pm
Waterfront Island Dining & Tiki Bar

If you're in the mood for a delicious burger, look no further. These big, juicy, made to order handhelds, all built with a custom blend of ground beef, are the "Reel" deal. Stand-outs include the classic "Backyard BBQ " burger with American cheese, LTO, sweet pickles, and Applewood smoked bacon, and the "Black 'N Blue," heaped with caramelized onions, lettuce, Applewood smoked bacon and blue cheese. There's also a terrific house-made Portobello Burger, grilled or blackened "Catch of the Day," and a Cilantro-Lime Marinated Grilled Chicken sandwich. Fresh fish tacos, grilled jumbo shrimp, lots of great apps, and specialty Tiki & Craft cocktails make this tropical oceanside spot a fun place to chill.

SAL'S BALLYHOO'S RESTAURANT
97860 Overseas Hwy, (On the Median)
Key Largo, Fl 33037
305-852-0822; ballyhoosrestaurant.com
Daily 11 am – 10 pm
Fresh Seafood & Steaks with a Southern Twist

Housed in a quaint 1930s Conch House which was once part of an early fishing camp, this bustling Key Largo eatery serves up fresh local seafood along with prime steaks and hearty sandwiches. Great seafood specialties include local fish prepared "Meuniere" (sautéed with white wine): "Hemingway" (Parmesan encrusted, finished with crab meat and key lime butter); and "Lorenzo" (egg-washed, sautéed, topped with a crab cake and finished with bearnaise. The plump, juicy Sea Scallops are also a winner.

SENOR FRIJOLES
103900 Overseas Hwy (MM 103.9 Bayside)
Key Largo, Fl 33037
305-451-1592; senorfrijolesrestaurant.com
Daily 11am — 9 pm
"Fresh Mexican Dishes and Margaritas"
Excellent Mexican food, tasty, hand-crafted margaritas made with fresh lime juice and spectacular sunsets are de rigueur here where South Florida-style seafood and Mexican food collide. The salsa, guacamole, and chips are all made from scratch.

SNOOK'S BAYSIDE RESTAURANT & GRAND TIKI
99470 Overseas Hwy, Bayside (Southbound Lane)
Key Largo, FL 33037
305-453-5004; snooks.com
Daily 11 am – 10 pm
Beautiful Island Dining On The Water
This chandeliered Grand Tiki, with its flickering torches, lush plantings, and Sobe-like sofa lounges, is oh-so-chic! A big open-air dining area, 5,000 square foot patio, and multiple bars all have unobstructed water views & provide a ringside seat to the best sunset celebration in town. The fresh island-inspired cuisine is also first-rate, and all made to order.

SUNDOWNERS
103900 Overseas Hwy
Key Largo, Fl 33037
305-451-4502; sundownerskeylargo.com
Daily 11 am – 10 pm
"Locally Caught Fish & Spectacular Sunsets"
The only thing better than the fresh, locally caught fish here is the unbelievable sunset. Great bread bowl soups, salads, sandwiches, and apps along with all sorts of interesting fish preparations. There's also a good selection of steaks, ribs, chicken, and vegetarian dishes.

TIDES BEACHSIDE BAR & GRILL
Islander Resort
82100 Overseas Hwy (MM 82.1 Oceanside)
Islamorada, Fl 33061
305-664-2031; islanderfloridakeys.com
Daily 11am - 11pm
Casual Beach Hang
A casual, Keysy menu and spectacular oceanfront setting make this poolside hang a perfect spot for chillin' with your favorite tropical libation. The all-day menu includes standard favorites including soups, salads, pizzas, burgers, and sandwiches along with signature plates like Mango Shrimp Tacos, House Smoked Wahoo Pate, Brick-Roasted Chicken, and Steak Frites.

ZIGGIE & MAD DOG'S
83000 Overseas Hwy (MM 83, Bayside)
Islamorada, FL 33036
305-664-3391; ziggieandmaddogs.com
Open Nightly 5 – 10 pm
Fri & Sat 'till 11 pm
Best Steak House In the Keys
Revived in 2005 by former Miami Dolphins' tight end and sports broadcaster, Jim "Mad Dog" Mandich and longtime business partner, Randy Kassewitz. The legendary Ziggie's Crab Shack is now sleek and sophisticated steak, chops, and seafood restaurant that feels more like Tommy Bahama than Ernest Hemingway. The current and now famous incarnation is better than ever and has become THE place for fine dining in the Keys. Orchid garnished cocktails, international wines, an outstanding a-la-carte menu, and nightly specials make it one of the Keys' top dining spots, which always draws a colorful celebrity clientele.

MARATHON/LOWER KEYS

7 MILE GRILL
1240 Overseas Hwy
Marathon, Fl 33050
305-743-4481; sevenmilegrill.com
Daily 7 am - 9 pm
You Can't Beat the Greek
This historic landmark is home to longtime restaurateur, Pete Chekimoglou, who serves up great local seafood along with unbelievably good Mediterranean dishes. The Gyros, Spinach Pie, and Greek Burger are amazing, and all the desserts are baked on-premises.

Keys Eats

BOBALU'S SOUTHERN CAFE
301 Overseas Hwy
Big Coppitt, Fl 33040
305-296-1664; bobalusrestaurantandbar.com
Tu - Sa 11 am - 9:30 pm; Open Su 11 am – 8 pm (Jan - March)
Comfort Food At Its Best
Located just a few miles outside of Key West, Bobalu's is renowned for its home-style cooking, New York-style pizza, and fresh local seafood. A new larger menu includes house-made Conch Fritters, Caribbean Pork Shanks, a Grouper Reuben, BBQ Pork Sandwiches, whole Yellowtail Snapper, Key West Pink Shrimp, and a lot of other tasty comfort food.

BOONDOCKS GRILLE & DRAFT HOUSE
27205 Overseas Hwy
Ramrod Key, Fl 33042
305-872-4094; boondocksus.com
The Keys Largest Tiki Bar
Whether you're a Shot-Guy, a Martini-Girl, or a Beer-Man, this monster Tiki Hut is always a fun place to hook up with other party lovers. Consistently good food is also a draw, and the restaurant has a vast selection of sandwiches and dinner entrées, including fresh catch baskets, artisan-crafted pizzas, crisp quality salads, huge burgers, and more.

BURDINE'S WATERFRONT
1200 Oceanview Ave (End of 15th St)
Marathon, Fl 33050
305-743-9204; burdineswaterfront.com
Daily 11 am - 9 pm
Casual Keys Fare
Burdine's is a laid-back, open-air Chiki Tiki Bar & Grille, overlooking Boot Key Harbor Waterway. They serve up very fresh casual Keys fare. Kudos to the two-fisted burgers and Big Biker Sausage, but serious foodies will appreciate the free-roaming 100% natural chicken dishes, organic spring mix salads, and delicious local fish.

BUTTERFLY CAFÉ
Tranquility Bay Resort
2600 Overseas Hwy
Marathon, Fl 33050
305-289-7177; tranquilitybay.com
Nightly 6 - 9 pm
Award-Winning Tropical Cuisine
Capturing the essence of island cuisine, this small cafe has a seafood-centric menu that changes seasonally. Popular items like Shrimp Pomodoro, Shrimp Cocktail, Crab-Stuffed Snapper, and a Cowboy Rib Eye are always spot-on. One thing that's always on the menu is the TDF - "To Die For" Sticky Toffee Pudding. And man is it ever!

CASTAWAY WATERFRONT RESTAURANT & SUSHI BAR
1406 Ocean Ave (MM 48, Oceanside)
Marathon, Fl 33050
305-743-6247; castawayfloridakeys.com
Daily 8 am – 10 pm
Good Comfort Food
Don't be surprised if a family of manatees drops by during mealtime at this popular waterfront eatery. Located on a small canal tucked off the Overseas Hwy, it serves up a wide variety of fresh, local seafood, steaks, and sushi with indoor or outdoor seating. They also have 54 beers on tap. FYI: Save room for Castaway's signature donut served with honey.

FISH TALES MARKET & EATERY
11711 Overseas Hwy
Marathon, Fl 33050
305-743-9196; floridalobster.com
Boat-to-Table Seafood
M - F 10 am - 8:30pm
It ain't big, and it ain't fancy, but when it comes to the freshest, tastiest seafood around, this family-owned and operated Marathon landmark is the real deal. A unique menu with Florida-inspired plates, original signature dishes, and lots of daily specials keeps the place packed with locals and in-the-know visitors. Great selection of German and craft beers on tap along with a terrific retail market with fresh fish, meats, and Certified Hand-Cut Angus Beef. Keep this one in your back pocket!

FLORIDA KEYS STEAK & LOBSTER HOUSE
3660 Overseas Hwy
Marathon, Fl 33050
305-743-5516; flkeyssteakandlobster.com
Daily 11:30 am – 10 pm
Great Food & A Bustling Bar Scene
This local's favorite, which is ALWAYS busy, is a Middle Keys mainstay. Although the menu is huge and varied (they even have made-to-order sushi and sashimi!), the food is always consistent and also includes great daily specials. Bar Manager/Mixologist, Sidney, makes the best classic cocktails in the Middle Keys, as well as a host of yummy concoctions that keep the barstools full all day.

FRANK'S GRILL
11400 Overseas Hwy
(MM 52 Gulfside - Town Square Mall)
305-289-7772
M - F 10 am – 3 pm; 5 – 9 pm; Sa 5 – 9 pm
Highly Acclaimed Old-World Italian
Frank Farello's highly acclaimed breakout venture embraces his family's Old World Italian recipes is also highly regarded for the great American and Classic Italian dishes, as well. Every dish is hand-crafted by Frank himself and includes signature favorites like Snapper Francaise, Veal Piccata, Chicken Marsala, Steak Roma, Shrimp Scampi, over a dozen pasta dishes, and all kinds of delicious fresh fish preparations.

HAVANA JACK'S
401 E Ocean Dr (MM 53.5)
Key Colony Beach, FL 33051
305-743-4849; HavanaJacksOceanside.com
Daily 11 am - Midnight
Spectacular Oceanfront Restaurant & Bar
With the cool mood of the Caribbean, this dramatic oceanside tiki restaurant and bar serves up tasty American/Caribbean fare and tropical libations against the panoramic backdrop of the Atlantic. You'll find a friendly crowd here, high-energy entertainment, indoor and outdoor dining, along with an elegant outdoor patio great for kickin' back. Call for free pick-up and drop-off anywhere on Key Colony Beach!

HERBIE'S BAR & CHOWDER HOUSE
6350 Overseas Hwy (MM 50.3, Gulfside)
Marathon, Fl 33050
305-743-6373; herbiesrestaurant.com
W - Su 11 am – 9 pm
Marathon's Oldest Operating Restaurant
This "big little restaurant" has been around for over 40 years and prides itself on preparing every dish from scratch — meaning it's fresh and local and as in-season as possible. Great fish sandwich, as well as chowders, burgers, and steaks. Bring your own fish, and they'll prepare it for you fried, blackened or grilled. Prices are good, too.

ISLAND FISH CO
12648 Overseas Hwy
Marathon, Fl 33050
305-743-4191; islandfishco.com
Daily 8 am — 10 pm
Waterfront Cheeky Tiki
Kick back with a frozen cocktail at the Keys' longest tiki bar where an intoxicating view of the Gulf transports you to Margaritaville. Open-air dining and a "Keysy" menu including items like Crabmeat Stuffed Shrimp, Crab Cakes, Conch Fritters, Burgers, and locally caught seafood. FYI: On Sunday, there's a special Mexican lunch menu.

KEY COLONY INN
700 West Ocean Dr (MM 53.5)
Key Colony Beach, FL 33051
305-743-0100; kcinn.com
Open Daily for lunch & dinner
Award-Winning Local Favorite
The big "Cheers" type bar here, with its old-time country club atmosphere, is a favorite locals' hangout. The diverse menu includes 75 Italian, fresh seafood, and continental specialties. The weekend Prime Rib Special always draws a big crowd. A popular spot for weddings and special events. FYI: The high season Sunday Brunch is exceptional.

KEYS FISHERIES SEAFOOD MARKET & MARINA
3502 Gulfview Ave
Marathon, Fl 33050
866-743-4353; keysfisheries.com
Daily 11 am — 7 pm; Market 9 am — 7 pm
Fresh Off the Dock Seafood
Come by boat, car, or your favorite mode of transportation for a casual bite on the fishing docks of this working marina. The menu is dominated by fresh, locally caught seafood (surprise, surprise). House Specialties like Corn Chowder, Conch Fritters, Lobster Reuben, Grilled MahiMahi, Hog Fish Francaise, and Jumbo Crab Claws (in-season). No table service but a fun Walk-up Window.

LIGHTHOUSE GRILL
Faro Blanco Hyatt Resort
1996 Overseas Hwy
Marathon, FL 33050
305-743-9018; faroblancoresort.com
Open M-Th 10 am – 11 pm;
Su 11 am - 11pm; F & Sa 11 am - 1 am
Outstanding Food & Views
Breathtaking views, gorgeous sunsets & an eclectic menu of fresh seafood, local favorites, and inspired daily specials, make this unique waterfront restaurant and tranquil veranda bar an excellent respite

Keys Eats

for a casual lunch, generous cocktails or romantic dinner. Located at Marathon's newly revitalized landmark, the Faro Blanco Resort, the Lighthouse Grill raises the bar for great dining in the Middle Keys.

LITTLE PALM ISLAND

Little Palm Island Resort & Spa
28500 Overseas Hwy (Oceanside)
Little Torch Key, Fl
305-872-2551;
littlepalmisland.com
Lunch M-F 11:30am – 2:30pm; Dinner Nightly 6 – 10pm
Put This One On Your Bucket List

After being completely wiped out by Hurricane Irma, this glam island resort is now back and better than ever. Little Palm is located just off the mainland. The lush, private island is dotted with thatch-roofed cottages, crushed seashell paths, and exotic wildlife. It's also home to one of the most fantastic dining experiences in the Florida Keys. FYI: Sunday Brunch here is just incredible.

LOOE KEY TIKI BAR

27340 Overseas Hwy
Ramrod Key, Fl
(305) 872-2215; looekeytikibar.com
11 am – 11 pm
Favorite Local Haunt

The food may not be fancy, but this favorite open-air haunt of Lower Keys locals is especially rockin' on Fri & Sat when there are live entertainment and dancing. You can graze through a casual menu that includes Chicken Wings, Wood-Fire Crust Pizza, and House-Made Chili or chow down on a big Tiki Bar Burger, Philly Cheese Steak, Grandma's Meatloaf or Chicken-Fried Steak. FYI: The Weds night Karaoke here is always a hoot.

MANGROVE MAMA'S

19991 Overseas Hwy
Sugarloaf Key, Fl
305-745-3030; mangrovemamas20.com
Th - M 11 am – 8 pm
Funky Landmark Restaurant & Bar

What was initially built in the early 1900s as a rail stop and residence for station agents eventually morphed into this funky, one-of-a-kind landmark. Today, it's a treasured watering hole for locals who like to swap stories under the banana trees and coconut palms. High-lights include the Smoked Fish Dip, Blackened Mini Tacos, Cuban paella, and plantain-crusted Hogfish.

MY NEW JOINT

At The Square Grouper
22658 Overseas Hwy
MM 22.5 Oceanside
Cudjoe Key 33042
305-745-8880; mynewjoint420lounge.com
T-Sa 4:20 - Midnight
Happy Hour 4:20 - 6:30 pm
Because Two Joints Are Better Than One

Head upstairs at The Square Grouper, and you'll discover a swanky bar and lounge (also known as SqGr2) where you can sip on hand-crafted specialty cocktails, graze on an innovative tapas menu, enjoy a fabulous raw bar, and indulge in yummy desserts. If you're a suds aficionado, you'll appreciate their unique tap system with 15 different draft beers plus a whopping 170 bottled beers. Lots of exciting wines, too, and all of them are available by the glass or by the bottle. A fun hang!

NO NAME PUB

30813 Watson Blvd.,
Big Pine Key, Fl
305-872-9115; nonamepubstore.com
Daily 11 am – 10 pm
Worth the Drive

Located off the beaten path, this rustic little spot is worth tracking down. The history of the No Name Pub dates back to 1931 when it was just a general store and bait & tackle shop. It remained that way until 1936 when the owners added a small room onto the main structure and turned it into a restaurant and pub. With walls now plastered with autographed dollar bills, the place is still rustic, funky, and fun after all these years. Add the draw of its Gourmet Pub Pizza, Homemade Conch Chowder, Smoked Fish Dip, and Stacked Pub Burgers — all served on paper plates, and we think you'll agree that this Lower Keys hideaway is worth the drive.

PORKY'S BAYSIDE

1410 Overseas Hwy (MM 47.5, Gulfside)
Marathon, FL 33050
305-289-2065; porkysbaysidebbq.com
Open M-Su 8 am – 10 pm
Daily Happy Hour 3 - 6 pm
Real Deal Southern BBQ On The Waterfront

An old Keys island vibe, "real deal" house-smoked BBQ & fresh oysters & sushi, and local seafood are the hallmark of this funky open-air waterfront hangout that always draws a big local crowd. There are terrific nightly specials along with homemade desserts, a great daily Happy Hour with the best mojitos in town, and live entertainment. You can even rent a jet ski or book an eco-tour here. Pet friendly, too!

SPARKY'S LANDING
MM 53.5, Oceanside
Behind the Holiday Inn Express
Key Colony Beach, FL 33051
305-289-7445; sparkyslanding.com
Open Daily 11 am — 10 pm
Great Wood-Fired Pizza
Fresh-off-the-boat fish, wood-fired gourmet pizzas, and generous cocktails rule the day at Matt and Carolyn Anthony's friendly, neighborhood dockside hangout. A big bar and open-air dining area overlooking the marina makes it a perfect spot to kick back and enjoy casual eats as well as fresh, local seafood and hearty flame-grilled steaks and chicken.

SQUARE GROUPER BAR & GRILL
2268 Overseas Hwy (MM 22.5, Oceanside)
Cudjoe Key, FL 33042
305-745-880; squaregrouperbarandgrill.com
Lunch 11 am - 2:30 pm
Dinner 5 – 10 pm
Cocktail Lounge 4:20 - Midnight
Not To Be Missed
A well-executed, inventive menu makes this unassuming roadside spot one of the Keys' top picks. Two cozy dining rooms, deliciously splashed with apple green and mandarin orange walls, set the stage for wonderful dishes like the Yellowfin Tuna and Avocado Egg rolls, Flash Fried Conch, Seafood Pasta with key lime butter sauce and other heavenly delights. Upstairs you'll find "My New Joint," a swanky cocktail lounge, tapas, and raw bar that's open 'till midnight.

SUNSET GRILLE & RAW BAR
7 Knights Key Blvd
Marathon, Fl 33050
305-396-7235; sunsetgrille7milebridge.com
Daily 8 am — 10 pm
Bring Your Swim Suit
Located right at the base of the 7 Mile Bridge (north side), this trendy oceanfront restaurant looks like a large thatched tiki hut and boasts one of the largest pools in the Keys. Multiple bars, live music, and a big, casual menu draw a party crowd — especially at Sunset when that big orange ball begins to drop into the Gulf.

KEY WEST

A&B LOBSTER HOUSE
700 Front St, Key West
305-294-5880; aandblobsterhouse.com
Top-Notch Dining with a Million Dollar View
This upscale fish house has been a popular Key West landmark since 1947. Delivered daily, the super fresh seafood here is excellent, as are the Certified Prime Black Angus steaks. Dine outside on the wrap-around porch for great views of the boats docked at Key West Bight.

ABBONDANZA ITALIAN RESTAURANT
1208 Simonton St.
305-292-1199; abbondanzakeywest.com
Daily 5 - 11 pm
Now That's Italian
Extra-large portions of standard Italian fare, family-friendly prices, and a relaxed, casual atmosphere have made this a favorite Key West dining destination and winner of the People's Choice Award for "Best Italian Restaurant." You'll find all of your favorites here, along with a delicious selection of seafood items and nightly specials.

ALONZO'S OYSTER BAR
700 Front St
305- 294-5880; alonzosoysterbar.com
Seafood and Sea Views Since 1947
Daily 11 am - 10 pm
Located smack dab on the docks of the Key West Bight in Old Town, this old-time favorite boasts the largest selection of cold and warm water oysters on the island. Dine outside with a view of Key West Bight and try the oysters, clams or shrimp served steamed or chilled, or any other seafood dish from the extensive menu. FYI: Appetizers are half-price during the daily happy hour.

Keys Eats

AMBROSIA
1401 Simonton St.
Key West, FL 33040
305-293-0304;
ambrosiasushi.com
Lunch M-Sa 11:30 am - 2 pm
Dinner M-Su 6 - 10 pm;
Key West's Best Sushi
A dramatic sculptured waterfall and ultra-cool sake bar provide a stunning backdrop for this island hot spot where authentic, artfully crafted plates take center stage. Chef/Owner Masa rocks the house with his premium blue fin tuna creations, signature rolls, sushi & sashimi while the kitchen serves up excellent Japanese specialties. Top it off with an eclectic selection of artisan sake and imaginative "Sake-tinis."

AMIGOS TORTILLA BAR
425 Greene St.
305-292-2009; amigostortillabar.com
Great Mexican Street Food
This casual street-side eatery is far from your typical taco stand. Amigos' handmade corn tortillas, which have no preservatives, trans or saturated fats, are overstuffed with seasoned meats, veggies, or fresh seafood and then topped with fresh-prepped diced onions, chopped cilantro, pico de gallo and salsas. And because the tortillas are square instead of round, there's less spilling and more filling.

ANTONIA'S
615 Duval St
Key West, Fl 33041
305-294-6565; antoniaskeywest.com
Daily 6:30 – 11 pm
An Authentic Taste of Italy
Outstanding regional Italian cuisine has made this cozy downtown cafe the darling of several national Food and Travel magazines. Hand-crafted pasta, seafood specialties, and hearty carne selections like Ossobuco and Rack of Lamb Chops please every palate.

AZUR RESTAURANT
425 Grinnell St
Key West, Fl 33041
305-292-2987; azurkeywest.com
Brunch Daily 9 am — 3 pm
Dinner Nightly 5:30 - 10 pm
Innovative Mediterranean
Tucked away in the heart of Old Town, is this low-keyed gem of a restaurant where you can get terrific Mediterranean fare on a shaded terrace by a waterfall or in the comfort of the relaxed dining room. The menu changes seasonally, with highlights like pan-seared yellowtail snapper over sautéed Swiss chard, with jumbo pink shrimp. Eggplant chips topped with salt and rosemary honey, and a whole grilled Bronzino fish served with rosemary, garlic, cured tomatoes, and Kalamata olives.

BAD BOY BURRITO
316 Petronia St
Key West, Fl 33040
305-292-2697; badboyburritokeywest.com
Daily 11 am — 8 pm
Gourmet - Style Burritos
Recently featured on the Food Network, this local favorite is your "go-to" spot for authentic Mexican food in the Keys. Hot, salty, sweet Kobe Beef Burritos, Surf N' Turf Tacos, and melt-in-your-mouth carnitas are all made with fresh local ingredients.

BAGATELLE
115 Duval St
Key West, Fl 33040
305-296-6609; bagatellekw.com
Daily 9 am – 10 pm
Tropical Seafood Fare
Located in a stunning 1800s Victorian and just a stone's throw from the world-famous Mallory Square, this long time favorite is known for its fresh seafood with a tropical flair. High-Fives to the Shrimp, Lobster, and Mussels over fettuccine, Swordfish Risotto, and the Lollipop Lamb Chops. FYI: The Lobster Mac n' Cheese is a real winner, too.

BANANA CAFÉ
1215 Duval St.
Key West, Fl 33040
305-294-7227;
bananacafekw.com
Daily 7:30 am –
10 pm
French Bistro With a Caribbean Twist
The food at this casual, cozy bistro is not only influenced by French cooking techniques but also by the local flavors of Southern Florida and the Caribbean. The

kitchen emphasizes fresh, local ingredients throughout the menu, which includes a good selection of sweet or savory crêpes, as well as crisp salads, hearty sandwiches, and a vast array of fresh local seafood prepared with a host of sauces. FYI: The Classic Baked Escargot with parsley-lime-garlic butter is out of this world.

BETTER THAN SEX: A DESSERT RESTAURANT
926 Simonton St.
Key West, Fl 33040
305-296-8102; betterthansexdesserts.com
Th - Tu 6 - Midnight
Desserts to Die For

For a decadent and romantic way to spend your night in Key West, check out this adult dessert-only restaurant. Sinful concoctions like "My Red Velvet Sheets Cheesecake," "Cookie Nookie Pie," and "Fork - You Fondue," — vanilla cheesecake fondue served chilled and paired with pound-cake doughnut holes rolled in cinnamon sugar will blow you away.

BISTRO 245
Opal Resort & Marina
245 Front St.
Key West, FL 33040
305-294-8320; bistro245.com
Daily 7 am-10 pm
Best Sunday Brunch

Bistro 245's top culinary team creates exceptional Caribbean cuisine on Key West's scenic harbor front. You can enjoy breakfast, lunch, or dinner comfortably indoors or dine casually outside Margaritaville Resort's Sunset Pier, which comes alive each evening with fantastic entertainment by the famous sunset performers. Award-winning Sunday Brunch with complimentary champagne from 10 am - 2 pm.

BLACKFIN BISTRO
918 Duval St
Key West, FL 33040
305-509-7408; blackfinbistro.com
Daily Brunch 11 am — 4 pm; Dinner 5 – 10 pm
Classic Neighborhood Bistro

The focus here is on simple food and fresh, locally-sourced fish. This sleek classic bistro serves up a well-rounded menu that includes Andalusian Gazpacho, an excellent Charcuterie Plate, Steamed PEI Mussels, lots of salads, Burgers, and Pasta dishes as well as several daily specials.

BLUE HEAVEN
729 Thomas St
Key West, Fl 33040
305-296-8666; blueheavenkw.com
Daily 8 am - 10:15 pm
Funky Key West Landmark

Opened by a pair of free spirits, Suanne and Richard, this Key West icon in historic Bahama Village has become a destination unto itself. It truly is funky alfresco dining with canopies of tropical foliage, improvised art, and a sail strung between trees providing shade. The chickens and cats roaming the premises have become almost as famous as the food. One taste of the Blueberry Pancakes, Carrot and Curry soup, Miso-Marinated Eggplant Salad, or Scallops Provençale, and you'll not doubt that fresh ingredients and the gentle time it takes to prepare fine food are the priorities. The menu barely ever changes, but it is oh-so-good. Get there early or be prepared to wait.

BOAT HOUSE BAR & GRILL
231 Margaret St
Key West, FL 33040
305-294-9191; commodorekeywest.com
Daily 11 am -10 pm; Happy Hour 4 - 6 pm
Casual Dockside Eats

With its nautical flags and rope-wrapped bar, this bustling dockside eatery captures all the charm of Key West's Historic Seaport and serves up an excellent and very affordable menu of salads, sandwiches, seafood, and steaks. During the daily Happy Hour from 4 - 6:30 pm, you can get 1/2 priced drinks and apps.

BO'S FISHWAGON
801 Caroline St
Key West, Fl 33041
305-294-9272; bosfishwagon.com
Home of the "Square Grouper Sandwich

A true slice of old Key West, BO's Fishwagon is about as real as it gets. As the name suggests, BO's Fish Wagon does its business from the inside of a wagon. Owner Buddy Owen has been handling his famous little hole in the wall for years, serving fresh conch and his signature sandwich: fried grouper with hot sauce. On Friday, B.O.'s Fishwagon opens up the stage for a live jam session.

COMMODORE RESTAURANT
231 Margaret St
Key West, FL 33040
305-294-9191; commodorekeywest.com
Open nightly 5:30 – 11 pm
Highly Acclaimed Steak & Seafood

Located on the docks of Key West's Historic Seaport, this highly acclaimed steak and seafood restaurant is consistently good and makes a perfect perch for breathtaking sunsets. A variety of choice cut meats, fresh, local fish, and an international wine list are all first-rate.

Keys Eats

THE CAFÉ
509 Southard St
Key West, Fl 33041
305-296-5515; thecafekw.com
Daily 9 am — 10 pm
Vegetarian & Vegan-Friendly Eats
"Roc the Veg" at this artful little chill spot in Old Town Key West. The Cafe is mostly vegetarian, serving delicious and fresh dishes with vegan and gluten-free options. Noteworthy: The veggie burger (house-made with legumes, carrots, broccoli, mushrooms, scallions, and sunflower seeds) is the bomb.

CAFÉ MARQUESA
Marquesa Hotel
600 Fleming St
Key West, Fl 33040
305- 292-1919; marquesa.com
Nightly 6 - 10 pm
One of Key West's Best
The contemporary American cuisine at this top-rated dining destination changes seasonally but always includes specialties like porcini-dusted diver sea scallops, served with mushroom truffle butter, herb risotto, and Swiss chard, as well as grilled black Angus filet mignon encrusted with a blue-cheese crust.

CAFE SOLE
1029 Southard St
Key West, Fl 33040
305-294-0230; cafesole.com
Open nightly 5 – 10 pm
Innovative, Award-Winning Menu
You'll think you've stumbled off the sidewalk and into Provence when you step inside Cafe Sole and catch the scents of fresh herbs and sautéed garlic. Chef/Owner John Correa, is a master of seafood & French sauces, and his food is a whoop of earthy, sun-drenched flavor. Must-Tries: the Conch Carpaccio and Hog Fish Snapper.

CHICO'S CANTINA
5230 US 1
Stock Island/Key West, Fl 33041
305-296-4714; chicoscantina.com
Daily 11:30 am - 9:30 pm
Award-Winning Mexican Food
This Stock Island favorite cooks authentic Mexican cuisine with lots of choices for tacos, burritos, enchiladas, and fajitas. Signature dishes are worth exploring. We like the Fish Adobado - fresh local catch marinated in red chili purée and seasoned with garlic, herbs, and spices, wrapped in corn husks and grilled over an open fire. The Yucatan Style Grilled Pork Chops (center cut marinated in Achiote seasoning) are also excellent.

CHINA GARDEN WEST DOWNTOWN
531 Fleming St
Key West, Fl 33040
305-296-6177; chinagardenkeywest.com
Daily 11:30 – 10 pm
Traditional Chinese
The Cheng family has been serving traditional Chinese cuisine in Key West for over 25 years. You'll find all the usual dishes here, including chicken chow mein, General Tso's Chicken, Sweet and Sour Pork, Moo Shu Vegetables, Curry Shrimp, and Vegetable Lo Mein. Big portions are large enough to share, and they're always open during the holidays.

CHRISTOPHER'S AT LA TE DA
1125 Duval St
Key West, Fl 33040
305-296-6706; lateda.com
Dinner Nightly 6 - 10 pm
Key West's Most Entertaining Restaurant
A lot is going on at La Te Da, which houses a hotel, piano bar, terrace bar, restaurant, and cabaret. The restaurant has contemporary island-inspired cuisine, including sautéed Key West Yellowtail Snapper, Baked Crab Cakes, Shrimp Scampi, and Crispy Lacquered Duck.

CONCH REPUBLIC SEAFOOD COMPANY
631 Greene St
Key West, Fl 33040
305 -294-4403; conchrepublicseafood.com
Daily 11:30 am - Midnight
Biggest Rum Bar Between Miami & Cuba
This casual, Caribbean-influenced eatery anchors Key West's Historic Seaport and is one of the island's most popular stomping grounds. A huge raw bar selection and fresh local seafood is the specialty here, but there's also a good selection of pasta, steaks, and specials. Happy hour from 4 - 7 pm draws crowds of locals – especially on Fri. when the crowd often swells to three deep.

CROISSANTS DE FRANCE & LE BISTRO
816 Duval St
Key West, Fl 305-294-2624
305-294-2624; croissantsdefrance.com
Daily 7:30 am – 9 pm
"A Little Bit Of Paris In Key West"
With its award-winning cuisine, delectable baked goods, and hand-sculpted cakes, this intimate outdoor garden cafe is vintage Key West with the relaxed atmosphere of a French Bistro. Breakfast and lunch served all day. Signature dinners include Boeuf Bourguignon, Chicken Cordon Bleu, Fresh Catch, Vegetarian dishes, and nightly specials. Free delivery. Also located at 5620 MacDonald Ave, Stock Island. 305-916-5669.

DUFFY'S STEAK & LOBSTER HOUSE
1007 Simonton St
Key West, FL 33040
305-296-4900; duffyskeywest.com
Open Daily Noon - 11 pm
Casual Dining At Affordable Prices
Duffy's is the place to go for excellent, affordable, and casual family dining in the heart of Paradise. Renowned for their fresh Florida lobster and delicious steaks, Surf and Turf, famous Key West Conch Fritters, and without a doubt, one of the best Prime Ribs in town. Be sure to get there early because this popular spot fills up fast—full bar with great tropical drinks.

EL MESON DE PEPE RESTAURANT & BAR
410 Wall St - Mallory Square
Key West, Fl 33040
305-295-2620; elmesondepepe.com
Daily 11 am – 10 pm
Authentic Cuban Food
This family-owned and operated Cuban restaurant has been a Key West favorite for over thirty years, and it's one the island's top go-to spots for authentic Cuban cuisine. Must Tries: Camarones de Coco - fried coconut shrimp with pineapple marmalade; and Ropa Vieja - a traditional Cuban dish of shredded beef marinated in Creole sauce; FYI: Every night at sunset, the local Caribe salsa band strikes a chord, and you can dance the night away.

EL SIBONEY RESTAURANT
900 Catherine St
Key West, Fl 33040
305-296-4184; elsiboneyrestaurant.com
Daily 11 am - 9:30 pm
The Real Deal
El Siboney is one of the island's best Cuban restaurants, serving generous portions of affordable, traditional Cuban cuisine. Top Picks: the Cuban Mix sandwich, Slow Cooked Roast Pork, and the Fried Chicken, which is first baked and then deep-fried. FYI: The Paella Valenciana is also absolutely terrific but takes extra time to prepare, so make sure you order ahead. They also have a second location on Stock Island at 5501 5th Ave. 305-296-4184.

FIREFLY KEY WEST
223 Petronia St
Key West, Fl 33040
305-849-0104; fireflykeywest.com
Daily Brunch 10 am — 3 pm; Dinner 6 – 10 pm
Modern, Chef-Driven Cuisine
New American food with a Southern influence is the hallmark if this relaxed, chef-driven restaurant where food-forward executive chef, Michael Price, and his crew hit a high note with a modern, innovative fare. The menu changes frequently but always includes a titillating selection of Southern favorites. A wide variety of wines by the glass and specialty beers make this Bahama Village hang a perfect respite.

FIRST FLIGHT ISLAND RESTAURANT AND BREWERY
301 Whitehead St
Key West, Fl 33040
305-293-8484; firstflightkw.com
Daily 11 am – 11 pm
Sunday Brunch 10 am – 2 pm
Birthplace of Pan American World Airways

Located in the former Key West headquarters of Pan American World Airways, which first flew from Key West to Cuba. This locally owned gastro pub includes a beautiful garden dining area nestled under the canopies of two Strangler Figs, an inside dining room with Pan American memorabilia, and an indoor-outdoor crash bar made from an airplane wing. The restaurant's seasonal menu focuses on locally sourced seafood and house brew braised dishes and fresh seasonal ingredients. Though Pan American is now gone, you can still toast the first flights from Key West to Cuba

FISHERMAN'S CAFÉ
205 Elizabeth St
Key West, Fl 33040
305-900-6878; fishermanscafekeywest.com
Daily 7 am — 5 pm
The Flavors of Old Key West
You'll feel like you stepped back in time at this small nostalgic restaurant where you can indulge in old-time classics like Harvey's Johnny Cake smothered in cheese grits, peel and eat Pink Shrimp, and the flavorful Steak and Egg Sandwich. Other timeless favorites

Keys Eats

take on a more modern twist like the Lobster Enchilada Tacos with authentic island sauce (as seen on the Cooking Channel), and Black Bean Burger topped with avocado.

THE FLAMING BUOY FILET CO
424 Eaton St
Key West, Fl 33040
305-295-7970
Nightly 6 - 8:30 pm
Always Delicious & Fun
This "Only in Key West" restaurant and wine bar makes a statement on the hushed stage of a residential neighborhood. It is one part retro supper club, one part sassy corner bistro, and part highly personal whim. Inventive contemporary menu options include BBQ Danish Baby Back Ribs - spice-rubbed, slow-baked, and finished on the grill with jalapeño barbecue sauce, Red Thai Curry with Shrimp, and Mahi Mahi with Banana Salsa.

GOLDMAN'S DELI
2796 N Roosevelt Blvd
Key West, Fl 33040
305-294-3354; goldmansdeli.com
M - Sa 7 am — 4 pm; Su 7 am — 3 pm
Nationally Acclaimed
Hailed as one of America's top 20 bagel deli's, Goldman's serves up traditional scratch-made New York deli-style fare. The bagels are boiled and baked daily on-premises, and the bread is house-made, as well. Deli favorites include the chicken noodle and matzoh ball soups, hot corned beef and pastrami sandwiches, burgers, kosher franks, smoked salmon, and herring in wine or cream sauce.

THE GRAND CAFÉ
314 Duval St
Key West, Fl 33041
305-292-4740; grandcafekeywest.com
Daily 11:30 am - 11:30 pm
Outstanding Contemporary American Cuisine
Located in a breathtaking Victorian mansion, this gracious restaurant is renowned for its fine island dining. Enjoy truly memorable dishes in one of the intimate dining rooms or outside on the big wrap-around porch and garden where you can watch all of the action on Duval. Winner of Wine Spectator's Award of Excellence with over 450 different bottles and more than 20 wines by the glass.

HARD ROCK CAFE
313 Duval St
Key West, Fl 33040
Daily 11 am - Midnight
305-293-0230; hardrockcafe.com/key-west
"Casual Eats That Rock"
Get a ringside seat overlooking the action on Duval while you chow down on an excellent array of casual eats, including homemade nachos, wings, spring rolls, the legendary 10 oz. Burgers and rockin' dinner entrees like the BBQ ribs, fajitas, pasta, and grilled steaks. Be sure to check out the cool Rock tees and memorabilia at the Rock Shop, which opens daily at 10 am.

HOGFISH BAR & GRILL
6810 Front St
Stock Island/Key West 33040
305-293-4041;
hogfishbar.com
Daily 11 am - Midnight
Step Back in Time

Tucked away on the working waterfront of Stock Island, this real "locals" spot avoids the pretension and hype of the more touristy areas. Fresh seafood, strong drinks, panoramic waterfront views, outdoor dining, and plenty of local characters are all on the menu, but it's the food that garners the rave reviews. The restaurant only uses hogfish caught by local divers and does not substitute other fish when it's out. Be sure to try the signature fried hogfish sandwich with Swiss cheese, onions, and mushrooms on fresh Cuban bread. It's outa-sight!

HOG'S BREATH SALOON
400 Front St
Key West, Fl 33040
305-296-4222; hogsbreath.com
Daily 10 am – 2 am
Where Drinking is a Sport
You might not think that a rockin' place like Hogs Breath has delicious food, but then you would be sadly mistaken. Once you've tried the Conch Fritters, fresh Smoked BBQ, Chicken Tacos, or Black & Bleu Burger, all backdropped by great live music, and you'll be hooked.

HOT TIN ROOF
Ocean Key Resort & Spa
0 Duval St
Key West, Fl 33041
305-296-7701; oceankey.com
Sun Brunch 11:30am — 2:30pm Dinner Nightly 5 - 10 pm
Upscale Dining with a Stellar Sunset View
The understated elegance of this waterfront dining room makes it a perfect spot for romantic couples. A Pan-Latin menu, with Caribbean and tropical influences, includes small and large plates so you can graze tapas-style or dine on more traditional entrees. Dishes like the Key lime fish ceviche, paella, and caramelized grouper capitalize on the fresh local seafood. FYI: The Sunday Brunch here is delicious and includes unlimited Bloody Marys and Mimosas.

JIMMY BUFFETT'S MARGARITAVILLE
500 Duval St
Key West, Fl 33041
305-292-1435; margaritavillekeywest.com
Daily 11 am — 11 pm
Wasted Away Again
Yes, this is the original Margaritaville, and yes, Jimmy Buffett has played both inside the restaurant and also just outside the door on Duval Street. Head here for a famous Cheeseburger in Paradise, topped with American cheese, lettuce, and tomato, served with Heinz 57 and fries; stay for the great live music playing most evenings.

LAGERHEADS
0 Simonton St
Key West, Fl 33040
305-509-7444; lagerheadsbeachbar.com
Daily 10am - 8pm
Little Beach Bar Off the Beaten Track
It doesn't get more beachfront than this rustic little bump in the sand. Enjoy a cold beer or a cocktail with fresh fish tacos or conch ceviche, then pull up a beach chair or sit on a stool on the small porch of this tiki shack and stay for a front-row view of the sunset. Along with the bar and restaurant, Lagerheads offers lots of water sports, including boat rentals, fishing, snorkeling, sunset cruises, and a harbor ride aboard a custom-built 1962 Navy Whale Boat.

LA GRIGNOTE
1211 Duval St
Key West, Fl 33040
305 -916-5445; lagrignotecafe.com
Tu - Sa 7 am – 5 pm; Su 7 am – 4 pm
Authentic Artisan French Bakery & Bistro
The French-born owners of this artisanal bakery offer a wide assortment of bread, croissants, viennoiseries (pastries), galettes (buckwheat crust with savory fillings), and more — all made from scratch. They also serve sandwiches on fabulous homemade bread.

LATITUDES AT SUNSET KEY
Opal Resort & Marina
245 Front St
Key West, FL 33040
305-292-5300; sunsetkeycottages.com
Daily 7 am — 10 pm
Stunning Beachfront Restaurant
Within minutes, the free boat launch at The Margaritaville Key West Resort & Marina transports you to this spectacular restaurant on the island of Sunset Key. Enjoy outstanding island cuisine in the ultra-luxe indoor dining room overlooking the Gulf of Mexico or outside in the sand surrounded by flickering tiki torches. Reservations required. Major credit cards. Present ticket while dining for free parking.

LA TRATTORIA
524 Duval St
Key West, Fl 33040
305-295-6789;
latrattoria.us
Nightly 5 – 10 pm
A Taste of Italy

La Trat's original Historic Old Town location exudes a romantic bistro-style setting right in the heart of Duval Street. Yellowtail Snapper, Hogfish, and Mahi are locally caught and prepared with super fresh ingredients. Classic Italian favorites like the Pasta Bolognese, Veal and Chicken Piccata, Ossobuco, and Grilled Lamb Chops are all delicious and beautifully prepared. You can also enjoy the same great menu at their oceanside location, 3593 S Roosevelt Blvd overlooking the Atlantic.

LOUIE'S BACKYARD
700 Waddell Ave.
Key West, Fl 33040
305-294-1061; louiesbackyard.com
Daily 11:30 am — 3 pm; 6 pm — 10 pm
AfterDeck Bar 11:30 am — 1 am
A Gourmand's Playground
Located in a historic picture-perfect Victorian which sits directly on the ocean, this seafood-centric restaurant is a top destination for foodies. In addition to beautifully prepared local caught hogfish, grouper, snapper, and Key West "Pinks" Shrimp, Executive Chef Doug Shook also does a masterful job with excellent steaks, heirloom pork, double lamb chops, and free-range chicken. FYI: Get there early so you'll have time to enjoy cocktails at "The AfterDeck Bar," which sits only a transom higher than the open Atlantic.

Keys Eats

MANGIA MANGIA PASTA CAFE
900 Southard St.
Key West, FL 33040
305-294-2469; mangia-mangia.com
Daily 5:30 – 10 pm
Good Friends. Good Food. Good Wine.
Renowned for perfect fresh homemade pasta & made-from-scratch, herb-spiked sauces, this cozy trattoria is one of the Keys' best values and serves up pure, full flavors that are intoxicatingly good. Lots of grilled specialties here, too, along with beef, seafood, chicken, and vegetarian dishes. Excellent gluten/egg-free pasta options, including "Zucchini Zoodle Noodles." The seductive wine list features vintages dating back to the 1950s.

MATT'S STOCK ISLAND KITCHEN & BAR
At The Perry Hotel
70001 Shrimp Road
Key West, FL 33040
305-294-3939; perrykeywest.com
Daily 8 am — 10 pm;
American Coastal Comfort Food
"Simple, tasty and delicious" food is the mantra at this new Stock Island eatery that serves breakfast, lunch, and dinner. Local seafood is the star of the show with House Specialties that include a Lobster BLT, Snapper On The Half Shell Tacos, Crab Beignets, Catch Of The Day, and lots of other exciting preparations. A lineup of burgers, ribs, and steaks provides plenty of great options for carnivores, as well.

NINE ONE FIVE & POINT5
915 Duval St
Key West, Fl 33040
305-296-0669; 915duval.com
W - Su 11:30 – 4 pm; Nightly 5 – 11 pm
New Island Cuisine
Executive Chef, Brendon Orr, is well known in the community for creating artful combinations of fresh local fare and Caribbean spices with Asian influences and French technique. You'll find lots of shareable items on the menu like the Absurdly Addictive Asparagus, Caramelized Brussels Sprouts, and Sichuan Eggplant & Tofu. Main Plates include a big selection of house-made pasta, seafood, and steaks. Dine alfresco on the elegant Victorian-style patio, sit inside the artsy first-floor dining room and bar, or head upstairs to Point5 for light bites and craft cocktails. Whatever your mood, it's a great hang.

OLD TOWN MEXICAN CAFÉ
609 Duval St
Key West, Fl 33040
305-296-7500;
oldtownmexicancafe.com
M - F 11:30 am - 10:30 pm;
Sa & Su 11:30 am – 11 pm
Authentic Mexican & New Mexican Fare

The salsa at this prominent Mexican Café is a Key West must-have. It is so good that local grocery store Fausto's sells it by the tub. Chef/Owner Gail Brockway does a great job with her authentic Mexican and New Mexican dishes and makes everything from scratch. FYI: Don't leave here without ordering her famous Banana Enchiladas.

ONLY WOOD PIZZERIA TRATTORIA
613 1/2 (Rear) Duval St
Key West, Fl 33040
305-735-4412; onlywoodkw.com
Nightly 5:30 – 10 pm
The Real Deal
Everything on the menu at this charming little trattoria is scratch-made using authentic Italian ingredients. The owners both grew up in a small village in Napoletana, Italy, where they learned how to make pizza from the founder of the Italian Association Napoletana Pizzaoli. The duo imported a massive brick oven from Vesuvius that reaches 1000°, which is required for an authentic Neapolitan style pizza. You will enjoy lots of other Italian favorites, including homemade Gnocchi, fresh Fettuccine, Lasagna, meatballs, and Bolognese as well as fresh local seafood and daily specials. Just terrific!

ORIGAMI SUSHI BAR
1075 Duval St, Key West, Fl 33040
305-294-0092; sushibarorigami.com
Nightly 5:30 – 10 pm
A Local Key West Favorite
Sushi Master, Kyoto Wada, entices his dedicated local following with super fresh sushi and sashimi, traditional and inventive rolls, plus a variety of Asian specialties. If you are genuinely "sushi-serious," and if you like a casual small-town vibe, this is the place to go. FYI: the Conch Carpaccio, Spicy Tuna Sandwich, and Spider Roll with tempura-fried soft shell crab are all the amazing!

PEPE'S CAFE
806 Caroline St
Key West, Fl 33040
305-294-7192; pepeskeywest.com
Daily 7:30 am - 9:30 pm
Killer Breakfast
Locals have been flocking to this Old Town institution since 1909. And for a good reason: the house-made fare and hearty breakfasts are delicious and for Key West, fairly reasonable to boot. You can eat inside or outback under the trees where there's a full bar mixing up drinks with fresh-squeezed juices. Love the meatloaf and grilled cheese sandwiches here, and we're avid fans of "Thanksgiving Dinner Day" on Thursday when they dish out fresh roasted Turkey with all of the trimmings.

PRIME STEAKHOUSE
951 Caroline St
Key West, Fl 33040
305-296-4000; primekeywest.com
Nightly 6 - 10 pm
Cozy, Upscale Steakhouse
One of Key West's priciest restaurants also serves high quality, prime-aged beef, including a signature 24oz Bone-In Ribeye, big beefy Porterhouse, and a 10oz char-broiled Filet Mignon. Local seafood, lobster tails, oysters, Pork Tenderloin, and a lovely Bone-In Veal Chop are also on the menu along with a good selection of exciting starters (She Crab Soup is especially good). Make sure you order a side of the Truffle Macaroni & Smoked Gouda.

ROOSTICA WOOD-FIRE PIZZERIA
5620 MacDonald Ave
Stock Island/Key West, Fl 33040
305-296-4999; roostica.com
Daily 11 am — 10 pm
Authentic Neapolitan Pizza
Using only soft-grain flour, fresh yeast, water, and sea salt for the dough, these authentic Neapolitan pizzas are cooked in a 900° oak-burning oven, including classics like the Margherita with San Marzano tomatoes and Bufala Mozzarella. Roostica serves a big selection of specialty pies. You can also build your own from one of the creative topping options. Lots of Italian "Soul Food," too, along with great nightly specials.

SALTY OYSTER DOCKSIDE BAR & GRILL
At The Perry Hotel
70001 Shrimp Road
Key West, FL 33040
305-294-3939; perrykeywest.com
Daily 11 am — 11 pm;
Just Steps From The Dock
This is the perfect spot to enjoy casual snacks by the dock at sunset, creative cocktails by the pool, or frozen concoctions in a private cabana. A short, simple menu does the trick with perennial favorites like fresh Oysters and local Key West Pink Shrimp, Po' Boys, and Burgers. FYI: All food and premium libations are 50% off during the daily 4 - 6 pm Happy Hour.

SALUTE! ON THE BEACH
1000 Atlantic Blvd
Key West, Fl 33040
305-292-1117; saluteonthebeach.com
Daily 11:30 am — 9:30 pm
Lovely Beachside Cafe
Get a ringside seat on Higgs Beach at this highly acclaimed open-air eatery that is owned and operated by the folks from the award-winning Blue Heaven Restaurant in Key West's historic Bahama Village. The menu is not overly complicated, but it is extremely good with a lighter Caribbean-influenced take on simple Italian classics and local seafood. FYI: If you've got the kids with you, there's a public playground right next door.

SANTIAGO'S BODEGA
207 Petronia St
Key West, Fl 33040
305-296-7691; santiagosbodega.com
Daily 11 am — 10 pm
Global Tapas Bar
Located off the beaten path in historic Bahama Village, this charming tapas-style restaurant is a foodie favorite where you can nosh on more than 30 inventive tapas-style dishes, soups, and salads. Top picks include the Spicy Shrimp Bisque, Yellowfin Tuna Ceviche, Petite Rack of Lamb, and Roman Meatballs. FYI: Save room for dessert — the hot rum-soaked bread pudding is TDF! Tables typically fill up quickly, so make sure to reserve.

SARABETH'S
530 Simonton St
Key West, Fl 33040
305-293-8181
Daily 8 am — 2 pm; Dinner Tu - Su 5:30 - 8 pm
Classic American Fare
Sister to Manhattan's famous eatery, this James Beard award-winner offers a fresh, updated take on classic American Cooking. You can't beat the breakfast here, which includes extraordinary eggs and omelets, Almond-Crusted Cinnamon French Toast, Lemon Ricotta

Keys Eats

Pancakes, and swoon-worthy baked goods. Lunch is also excellent with offerings like the Open-Face Tuna Salad on garlic-rubbed grilled sourdough topped with fresh chopped tomatoes, marinated in aged balsamic vinegar, extra virgin olive oil, and basil. FYI: Sunday Fried Chicken night with house-made gravy is especially good.

SCHOONER WHARF BAR
200R Williams St.
Key West, FL 33040
305-292-3773; schoonerwharf.com
M - Th 8 - 2 am; F - Su 7:30 - 2am
The Last Remnant Of Old Key West
This funky, open-air waterfront bar sits on the docks overlooking the marina. The food and mood are Key West casual, and the menu has all your island favorites, including wings, nachos, burgers, fish tacos, seafood platters, conch fritters, pink shrimp, and more. Great live music and two daily Happy Hours from opening until Noon and then again from 5 - 7 pm.

SEVEN FISH RESTAURANT
921 Truman Ave
Key West, Fl 33040
305-296-2777; 7fish.com
Wed-Mon 4 - 8:30 pm
A Key West Classic
This intimate, seafood-centric restaurant has been going strong for more than twenty years and just seems to get better with age. The local seafood dishes are genuinely remarkable, and everything on the menu is scratch-made. There are lots of House Specialties with stand-outs like the Thai Curry Snapper, Banana Chicken, and 7 Fish Meatloaf - considered to be a local favorite.

THE STONED CRAB
Ibis Bay Beach Resort
3101 N. Roosevelt Blvd
305-443-9431; stonedcrab.com
Daily 10am - 11pm
Everybody Must Get Stoned
The Stoned Crab is the only restaurant in Key West that specializes in stone crab. They have two private fishing boats that deliver their catch, including "Key West Pinks," straight to the restaurant's dock each day. Spectacular dishes like the "Seafood Towers," Blackened Key West Shrimp & Grits, Stoned Crab Cakes, Seafood Pasta, and an array of other interesting plates are all noteworthy.

TAVERN N' TOWN
Marriott Key West Beachside Resort
3811 No. Roosevelt Ave.
Key West, FL 33041
305-296-8100; tavernntown.com
Open M - Su 8 am – 10 pm
World-Class Dining & Entertainment
Key West notables dine on a fusion of globally inspired tapas (small plates), designer pizzas, grilled meats, plancha seared fish, and nightly specials. If you sit directly in front of the vast "Tapas Theater Kitchen," you can watch the chefs work their magic, embellishing international favorites with the unique flavors of Key West. Daily 2 4 1 Happy Hour and special Tapas Nights every Tues & Thurs from 5 - 7 pm. Nightly entertainment.

WAHLBURGERS
700 Front St
Key West, FL 33040
305-433-2020; wahlburgers.com/keywest
Daily 11 am-10 pm
Casual Dockside Eats
Key West is the newest stomping ground for Mark Wahlberg, boy band brother Donnie, and executive chef, Paul. Their new 5,141 square foot restaurant and bar has tons of outdoor seating and an alfresco bar overlooking the Seaport and the A&B Marina. Like all of the Wahlburgers restaurants, the new Key West location includes lots of photos and memorabilia that capture the brothers' early days of growing up in the Dorchester neighborhood of Boston. In addition to their signature burgers, the menu also includes childhood favorites like tater tots, house-made chili, haddock sandwiches, Yukon French fries, bacon mac 'n cheese, fluffanutta sandwiches, and house-made shakes/floats.

INDEX

A&B Lobster House 89
Abbondanza 89
Alice Weingarten 13
Alonzo's Oyster Bar 89
Ambrosia Sushi & Sake Bar 24, 25, 90
Amigo's Tortilla Bar 90
A Moveable Feast 17, 81
Antonia's 90
Azur Restaurant 90

Bacon-Wrapped Love Meatloaf Recipe 42, 43
Bad Boy Burrito 90
Bagatelle 90
Banana Bread Recipe 68
Banana Café 90
Baygrass Bluegrass Craft Beer Festival 70
Beef Recipes 40, 42, 43, 55
Better Than Sex Dessert Restaurant 91
Bistro 245 28, 29, 91
Blackfin Bistro 91
Blue Heaven Restaurant 91
Boat House Bar & Grill 91
BO's Fish Wagon 91
Bobalu's Southern Café 86
Boondock's Grill 86
Burdine's Waterfront 86
Butterfly Café 86
Braised Short Ribs Recipe 40
Burrata Cheese Recipe 30, 31
Buzzard's Roost 36, 37, 81

Café, The 92
Café Marquesa 92
Café Sole 26, 27, 92
Castaway Waterfront Restaurant 86
Cheeca Lodge, Nikai 84
Chef Michaels 82
Chico's Cantina 92
Chipotle Glazed Mahi Mahi Recipe 37
Christopher's at La Te Da 92
Ciao Hound Italian Kitchen & Bar 48, 49, 81
Cilantro-Seared Swordfish 57
Conch Carpaccio 27
Conch Ceviche Recipe 13
Conch Chowder 21
Conch Egg Rolls Recipe 12
Conch Republic Seafood Co 92
Conch Salad 16
Croissants de France 93
Cuban Restaurants 93

David Sloan 66
Desserts 64, 65, 67, 68, 69
DiGiorgio's Café 82
Directions, Book 6

Duffy's Steak House 93

El Mason De Pepe Restaurant 93
El Siboney Restaurant 93
Espresso Glazed Bacon Recipe 15
Evangeline Washington 60

Faro Blanco Resort 56, 87
Filet Mignon Island Style Recipe 55
Firefly Key West 93
First Flight Island Restaurant 93
Fish House Restaurant & Seafood Market 38, 39, 82
Fish & Key Lime Butter Sauce Recipe 47
Fish Matecumbe Recipe 39
Fish Tales Market & Eatery 86
Fisherman's Cafe 93
The Flaming Buoy 94
Florida Keys Cuisine 4, 5
Florida Keys Holiday Festival 73
Florida Keys Island Fest 71, 77
Florida Seafood Festival 70
Florida Keys Steak & Lobster House 86
Foodie Happenings 70-79
Food Truck Festival 70
Frank's Grill 87
Fried Chicken 60
Frutti Di Mare Recipe 49

Gingerbread House Making Party 73
George Patti 40
Goldman's Deli 94
Green Turtle Inn 42, 43, 82

Handhelds & Lite Bites 7
Hard Rock Café 94
Herbie's Bar & Chowder House 87
Honey Glazed Citrus Salmon Recipe 56
Hog's Breath Saloon 94
Hogfish Bar & Grill 94
Honey Grilled Chicken Recipe 45
Hospice & VNA July 4th Picnic 72
Hot Tin Roof 95

Island Fish Co 87
Island Gazpacho 29
I Love Stock Island Festival 73
Islamorada Seafood Fest 71
Island Shrimp Cakes 61
Islander Resort 85

Jimmy Buffett's Margaritaville 95
John Correa 26

Kaiyo Grill & Sushi 62, 82
Key Colony Beach Day 71

INDEX

Key Colony Inn   50, 51, 87
Keys Conch Chowder   21
Keys Fisheries Seafood Market   87
Key Largo Chamber of Commerce Cook-Off   73
Key Largo Fisheries Backyard Cafe   8, 9, 82
Key Largo/Islamorada Uncorked   70, 74
Key Lime Festival   72, 79
Key Lime Pie Recipe   67
Key West Whiskey Fest   72
Key West Brewfest   72
Key West Food & Wine Festival   70, 75
Key West Lobsterfest   72, 80
King Crab Burger Recipe   11
Kristi's Tropical Rum Cake Recipe   64

La Grignote   95
La Te Da   92
Latitudes Restaurant   30, 31, 32, 95
La Trattoria   95
Lazy Days Restaurant   46, 47, 83
Lazy Lobster   68, 83
Lighthouse Grill   56, 87
Little Palm Island   88
Lagerheads   95
Looe Key Tiki Bar   88
Lorelei Restaurant & Cabana Bar   20, 21, 83
Louie's Backyard   95

Main Events   33
Mangia Mangia Pasta Cafe   58, 59, 96
Mango Fest Key West   65, 72, 78
Mango Pie Recipe   65
Mangrove Mama's   88
Mangrove Mike's   83
Mark Certonio   78
Marriott Beachside Resort   57
Master Chefs Classic   70
M.E.A.T.   40
Mile Marker 88   12, 83
Morada Beach Cafe & Bar   84
Mrs. Mac's Kitchen   84
My New Joint   88

Nikai   84
Noche Buena Christmas Eve Feast   73
No Name Pub   88

Old Town Mexican Cafe   96
Olive Morada   14, 15, 41, 64
Only Wood Pizzeria   96
Opal Resort & Marina   28, 29, 90
Original Marathon Seafood Festival   71, 74

Pamela Childs   103
Pasta Recipe   49, 59
Pepe's Cafe   67, 97

Pierre's Lounge & Restaurant   84
Pina Colada Shrimp Recipe   41
Porky's Bayside   22, 23, 88
Poultry Recipes   45, 60
Prime Steakhouse   97

Reel Burger   10, 11, 84
Restaurant Listings   81-98
Roostica Wood-Fire Pizza   97

7 Mile Grill   52, 53, 85
Sal's Ballyhoo Restaurant   84
Salty Oyster Dockside Bar & Grill   97
Salute On The Beach   97
Santiago's Bodega   97
Sarabeth's   97
Schooner Wharf Bar & Grill   54, 55, 98
Seafood Recipes   9, 11, 12, 13, 16, 19, 21, 23, 25, 27, 35, 37, 39, 41, 47, 49, 51, 53, 56, 57, 59, 61, 62
Señor Frijoles   85
Seven Fish Restaurant   98
Shaved Conch Salad   16
Smoked Fish Dip Recipe   23
Snook's Bayside   34, 35, 85
Socca Recipe   17
Soups   21, 29
Shrimp Burger Recipe   9
Shrimp Saganaki Recipe   53
"Spay-ghetti & No Balls" Holiday Gala   73
Sunday Brunch   36, 50, 90, 95
Sundowners   85
Sparky's Landing   89
Spicy Tuna Tartare Recipe   25
Tako-Yakini Ku Recipe   62
The Stoned Crab Restaurant   98
Sweet Treats   64, 65, 67, 68, 69
Swordfish Recipe   57
Square Grouper Bar & Grill   18, 19, 61, 88

Taste of Key West   72
Taste of the Islands   73
Tavern N Town Restaurant   57, 98
Tides Beachside Bar & Grill   85
Tropical Rum Cake Recipe   64

Uncorked Food & Wine Festival   70, 74

Valentine's Day Champagne & Aphrodisiacs Sunset Sail   70
Vegetarian Recipes   17, 29, 31

Wesley House Valentine's Day Gala   71

Yellowtail Snapper Recipe   35

Ziggie & Mad Dogs   44, 45, 85

Keys Eats is a labor of love by author Pamela Childs,
editor Karen Davis and art director/designer, Marsha Michaels
who have all been residents of the Florida Keys & Key West for decades.
The crew also publishes Destination Florida –
Florida's #1 Visitors Guide.
For more local recipes, happenings, restaurant reviews, sample menus
and more hit up DestinationFlorida.com.

Life here is so endlessly delicious…

If you want to discover where to indulge in good food and good times during your next Florida adventure, hit us up at DestinationFlorida.com.

DESTINATION™ FLORIDA

• Florida Keys & Key West • Greater Tampa Bay • St Pete • Sarasota • Clearwater • Cedar Key • Gainesville • Naples • Bonita Springs • Charlotte Harbor • Englewood Beach • Everglades • Fort Myers • Fort Myers Beach • Marco Island • Naples • Punta Gorda • Sanibel-Captiva • Daytona • Ormond Beach • New Smyrna • Port Orange • The Palm Beaches

About the Author
Pamela Childs

Before putting down roots in the Florida Keys, native Rhode Islander, Pamela Childs grew up in a home where the family kitchen table always held center stage. She credits her passion for all kinds of food to the culinary talents of her mom, who instilled in her a sense of love for the new, the tasty and the interesting. Now, after various careers in advertising, retail, hospitality and publishing that took her from Boston to Cape Cod to Key West, Pamela returns to the kitchen table and her love of a good meal with this fun compilation of her favorite Keys recipes and foodie hangouts.

Follow her at
DestinationFloridaKeys.com

DESTINATION™
FLORIDA

Find out more about the Florida Keys & Key West at
DESTINATIONFlorida.com

www.ingramcontent.com/pod-product-compliance
Lightning Source LLC
Chambersburg PA
CBHW051121110526
44589CB00026B/3001